The Trouble with Management

Stephen F. Green

Copyright © 2014 Stephen Green

All rights reserved.

ISBN:1503366952
ISBN-13:9781503366954

DEDICATION

To Heidi, my devoted wife, to all my family in the UK and Denmark and not least my dear departed brother, Peter.

CONTENTS

	Acknowledgments	i
1	Preface	iii
2	What's the Problem?	5
3	The Current Conundrum	23
4	The Road Ahead	66
5	Shaping the Environment	108
6	Trouble Averted	142
7	The Educational Imperative	176
8	Where does all this Lead?	194
9	Are we nearly there yet?	204
10	Getting there	212

ACKNOWLEDGMENTS

There are so many people I owe a great debt of gratitude. Either knowingly or inadvertently, they have contributed to the content and direction of the material contained within these pages. A study in Management is a study of us all.

Preface

There is no complete instruction manual for being a great Manager.
This is not an instruction manual.
There is no great template for every situation; no model for every circumstance.
This is neither a comprehensive model nor a template.
But perhaps, it might be the beginnings of one.

I would like it to be a direction or a pathway that anyone can take, no matter how far along the road they may find themselves. I am well aware that even this undertaking is open to misinterpretation and could well disappoint those who want all the answers. A guidebook is only useful if it reveals the possibilities of where to go; it can only be useful if the adventurer knows where they are. A guidebook, by its very nature, is not intended to be dogmatic but there is a line to tread between principle and discretion. My objective is not just to paint a simple picture of how things are but how they ought to be; not just the direction that has to be taken but a possible alternative.

What's the Problem?

Managers are left in impossible situations. If the truth was known, many of those situations are often of a Manager's own making. The actions and behaviours of *those in charge* can cause friction, tensions, misunderstanding, frustration and misspent energy. At times, the struggle can be exacerbating and baffling. The dilemma and quandary facing Managers in this day and age are no less than they have been for decades despite advancements in technology, data capture and communication services. The reality can be that strenuous efforts are made to engage and motivate a group of people that have, either unwittingly or deliberately, been coerced into submission, have been led into a climate of disengagement and restraint and have been left to their own devices when each vestige of creativity and enterprise has been extracted by an organisational syringe. 'Understanding the predicament', 'comprehending the circumstances', 'taking stock', possessing 'situational awareness' are not only the tools any accomplished business Manager needs – they are just as necessary in everyday life. And sometimes, those life skills are left at the door of the office.

There are reasons for this state of affairs - other factors pervade and play their part in shaping the environment with which a Manager has to contend. Within any organisation, perceptions and interpretations are reconstructed to create a perspective that can be divorced from the outside world. It is not always strikingly obvious and evident; it is not always the top of the agenda or the presiding subject of interest that arrests everyone's attention. Management is not just about dealing with people, it is also about dealing with the way organisations believe people should be 'dealt with'; it is about how the organisation wants people to *perform* and how Managers need to act and behave. This is not an excuse – just the everyday circumstances and the scale of what a Manager has to change not only about him or herself but about their peers, the environment, the conditions of work, the hierarchy, the systems, processes and structure of responsibilities.

If nothing else, the following chapters are about 'Change' – a change in the way Managers perceive themselves and are perceived by others within their chosen role. It is a role that can so often be misperceived, misunderstood and taken in all other directions than the one that is actually required. I aim to promote the idea that we need a fresh perspective on a subject that is too easily disguised in the paraphernalia of rank, authority and the inscrutability of leadership. It does require some soul-searching and contrite examination. But it also needs clarification. There is quite clearly some uncertainty and it is beyond doubt that this leads Managers to act as they do. Clarification lies in the task of finding 'where you are' before any change is attempted and 'how good' a

Manager you really are becomes critical and absolute in finding the best direction and way forward.

The problem is of course, that Management is synonymous with power and authority, rank and status. The text book definition answers the question Managers would like to hear - considered wisdom provides the answers that resonate and have the ring of truth. But this does not have to be the case. The context has to be examined and age-old principles challenged. It is not just about the Manager but about the very people for whom a Manager has responsibility. It is not just about doing well and individual achievement, it is about helping, supporting and inspiring others to achieve - those whose livelihoods, well-being and success a Manager has ultimate responsibility and accountability.

If you can't annoy somebody with what you write, I think there is little point in writing. Kingsley Amis.

I do not intend to propose a diametric, contradictory view. It is, after all, a subject that has been, in different ways, discussed for centuries. I do, however, believe this view may well be *different* - and it needs to be, otherwise there would be little value and little point. There always has to be an alternative way of looking at the world – even it is by a little degree. The disparity between perception and certainty may at times be fractional but the gap needs to be clarified as it invariably points in the direction one needs to take. Even more to the point, the digression from what should be done and what is actually practiced - how Managers truly 'manage' - is by far the greater step that needs to be understood and becomes an essential requirement of 'change'.

The written subject of Management has been a mirror of the times even though early writings on Management, advocating the ways and strategies for would-be leaders, still find their voice today. Management literature, in its most common form, has lost some of its bombastic, military and political clothing but there are still those who use *Sun Tzu,* the Chinese General's *Art of War* as a foundation on which to reap and conquer. The Indian *Arthashastra* covered the questions every aspiring leader needed to know: when to kill, when to spy, when to sacrifice, when to invade a neighbour and when to protect yourself from assassination from your own wife – all important and relevant stuff. The much-maligned Renaissance writer, Niccolo Machiavelli, who, in writing 'The Prince' aimed to infuse Leadership with an adamant and blunt approach to dealing with enemies and subordinates was just as uncompromising and pragmatic. It was cruel politics in a cruel world. Some of the first vestiges of humanity appeared in Erasmus's 'The Education of a Christian Prince' in which he argued for a Leader's inherent goodness and unimpeachable morality which should supersede ambition and political expediency. Recently, the pace and abundance of text books has multiplied, extrapolating this humanistic approach with a populist zeal to be more engaging and involving, though still extolling the virtues of strong, capable leadership. No matter their source, place and time, they all have a common denominator; they all have a common purpose.

All are obsessed with finding the 'right way', the 'correct method', the 'best ten learnings' and the 'twenty most effective measures' that would, if adopted, transform the reader from mediocrity to being a high-flier, from 'one in the crowd' to a cherished, charismatic leader. The self-help books fill the shelves with the accumulated acumen and fail-safe principles of achieving the success every reader feels they deserve. Understandably, authors hesitate to mention the apprenticeship, the years of trial and error, the mistakes, the disasters and the catastrophes. One could be easily be led to believe there was a starting point of excellence: an esoteric font of wisdom owned by a few and patronisingly distilled and filtered to the many. There are numerous "quick-fix" programmes and philosophies that lead to amazing Management profiles in a number of easy lessons without taking reality into consideration – making the expectant reader frustrated by the conflicting practicalities of their organisations and the role they are asked to play.

Many of the new testaments are attractive simply because there is a craving for success, advancement, promotion, reward and power - all of which are appealing and seductive. By reading, digesting and absorbing all the lessons on offer, the willing aspirant is cajoled into believing they can jump the queue of hopefuls; they can steal a march on the great unread and dazzle their superiors with new approaches and new wisdom. Each manuscript promises financial rewards and the trappings of respect, superiority, control and authority– all the things to which Management *alludes* but which are ultimately misconstrued, erroneous and manifestly misleading. They are traps that willingly distort the role of the present-day Manager. The truth is that 'Management' has a multitude of expressions and guises - alternate masks that people like to compress into a pastiche of learning.

The disparity between the 'big bad world' and the contents of any text book are evident and unmistakable. This is not to cripple any good intentions but irrespective of how it is viewed, the 'Ten Steps' to Management perfection becomes more of a study in encouragement and *wannabe* aspiration - inspirational techniques from practiced optimists who turn pen to paper and do everything but motivate and inspire. They are recondite learnings that leave everyone puzzled and none the wiser. Many readers, I am sure, find them fearfully condescending and inappropriate.

I have no hidden agenda or axe to grind. My motives are simply to present a re-adjustment of a commonly held and ingrained perspective. Whereas industry and business has changed, more importantly, *people* have changed. Not only in terms of social intelligence but also with the freedom and ability to think beyond the boundaries set by others. The reality, mis-represented in many Management theses, does not alter the simple unalterable fact: that no guru, professor, leader, Manager nor acolyte has a monopoly or divine righteousness to any individual point of view. Advances in human thinking may be considered millimetric but there is still an optimistic and relentless march to the truth regardless of the most conservative forces at work.

To create great leaders through the written word alone is fraught with difficulties and perhaps, opportunistic on the part of the author. For a reader to believe they can become a great Manager simply by reading a text book is like learning how to be a good racing driver in a classroom. There are many people with good, resonant messages which are delivered badly and never see the light of day and there are many strange and unbelievably bad messages presented well enough to be believed by the ambitious. And yet, there is legitimacy in them all: there is always one single snippet, one golden nugget, affirmations of fact and catalysts of certainty on almost every page. The fact is, you can pick up the most pedestrian monologue, the most trite article, the most mundane clip from You-Tube, the most considered and eloquent thesis and be forced to question, confirm, reconsider or re-evaluate that which each hold to be true.

There is no great alchemy in the production of young prodigies. Whereas each new piece of Management literature carries the weighty assertion of changing cumbersome leaden pieces into bars of gold, there needs to be a good measure of practicality – and sanity. There is no panacea and no sprinkle of magic that can transform the new starter to a superstar - there can only be direction and guidance, a path and a route-map that can steer each individual in the right direction. How quickly one can travel is up to diligence, good fortune, talent and application of some simple rules. And here lies the truth: it is not through equipment, gadgets, complex analysis and secret formulae but through simple human routines, disciplines and behaviours. This is not just about the individual Managers, it is also about the organisations in which they work. Organisations expect a lot from Managers but do not necessarily provide the framework by which they can perform effectively or achieve their potential. Lip-service is paid to *engagement; motivation* is done by paying bonuses; *development* is done through 'sending people on courses', and *conflict* is done by...well, by skirting the issue. To expect excellence in this sea of contradictions is bound to create a tide of disappointment.

It ain't what you don't know that gets you into trouble. It's what you know for sure that just ain't so. Mark Twain

Lee Iacocca, the former head of Chrysler and Ford, wrote that: "Management is nothing more than motivating other people". Succinct and simple. You wouldn't expect anything more, would you? But, is that it? If so, rather than go through hours of reading, lectures and interminable tutorials, would it not be better to pick up a copy of motivation techniques from the local book store? Wouldn't that be simpler? And if motivation - getting people to perform better, faster, more efficiently - is the only trick a Manager has up his or her sleeve, doesn't this negate and diminish the effort and complications of day-to-day management? Doesn't this avoid the thornier issues of power, authority, leadership and control? More importantly, isn't this an entirely management-centric way of looking at organisations and their place in the world? Does it not completely avoid the aspirations of the people we call workers, staff, Employees or subordinates?

Ideally the truth may well lie in the fact that that we have moved away from this archaic form of simplistic preaching: *'I am going to motivate you in ways you have never considered and in a direction you may or may not want to go'.* If not, then perhaps work is nothing more than an energetic training-session with some over-enthusiastic gymnast grunting instructions to get everyone animated and engaged; a purgatory of quick, juicy sound-bites, and mission statements that has everyone elated, enthused and 'valued'. The thought is dreadful and unappealing. Perhaps there are those who still believe that a ten-step motivational lesson from each Manager will transform lethargic and disinterested Employees into ecstatic individuals fighting in a joint cause for the greater good of the Company? That would be hopelessly naïve. 'Motivating people' is a narrow view of Management and one that belies not only the complexity of individuals on both sides of the Management divide but also the range of issues that have to be tackled. If a Manager's job is simply to motivate, what do they do once they have achieved this state of engaged nirvana? What about the finances, health and safety, the systems, processes and routines? What about strategy and values? What about Marketing, Sales and Procurement?

Are Managers really necessary?

We should not get ahead of ourselves. There is a simple supposition that is too easily overlooked and often too awkward to suggest. For every vehicle of entrepreneurial free enterprise, business and structure, comes an equally arbitrary conclusion that there ought to be at least one level of Management and several levels of Supervision. This stems from the supposition that 'ordinary' people – Employees - need to be governed, guided, instructed and manipulated in ways they could not conceive if left alone. This apparent conceit, whilst ubiquitous and self-serving, prepares the foundations for many misconceptions.

Despite what many like to believe and what others love to preach from diverse manuscripts of folklore, humans formed a workable, fabric of social morality and set of ethics before any Bronze Age scripture came into being. The very survival of our species has not only come about through simple, supportive rules and ways of working but also through a natural instinct for cooperation and achievement with one another - well before the advent of modern 'Management'. The world of the hunter-gatherer was not supervised, assessed, audited and financially controlled at any point of the process – the imperatives of life were far too immediate and the consequences of failure catastrophic. The great building works, from the ancients through the renaissance, whether inspired by a mystical deity or despot were hardly conceived by a gaggle of bureaucrats. And yet, from the 18th century onwards, a sweeping era of change brought about its own philosophy of keeping things under *control* and making sure that every penny spent on labour was examined by an increasing number of overseers, accountants, superiors and supervisors. The need for a Manager was not only a new invention, it satisfied a self-serving and well-articulated 'necessity'.

Hardly a competent workman can be found who does not devote a considerable amount of time to studying just how slowly he can work and still convince his employer that he is going at a good pace. Frederick W. Taylor

Frederick W. Taylor (1856 -1915) founded some enduring traditions in the field of Management and Management Consultancy. In his writings, he demonstrated the worst in human generosity and at the same time, conveyed the upmost contempt in the way that people scratched a living. To paraphrase, if people were stupid enough to do the menial jobs on offer, then they were not clever enough to consider how efficiently that work could be completed. Only a Manager could do that: someone versed in the technicalities of efficiency, expediency, decision making and profitability. If Taylor was at all correct in his assumptions, there was little explanatory evidence or empathy regarding the conditions in which people had to work, how they were paid and how they were treated as human beings. Equally, once there was an assumption that people need to be galvanised, exhorted, motivated, channeled and even forced to do 'what was required', there was an impulse to interfere, a need to cajole, a need to stimulate and a need to regulate.

There is a perception in the minds of even the highest placed executive that the machinery of production would grind to a steady halt with no Supervision or Management in place. Supposing this workplace 'Armageddon' was true, would that not pose a greater problem? Would it not be a greater indictment of current practice and the accepted state of affairs? Does it not cement the myth that running around at a breathless pace, attending endless meetings, sifting through inaccurate data, having a phone glued to each ear is key to keeping the whole organisational apparatus on an even keel? Would it not justify the common perception and depiction of every thoroughly modern Manager?

Is this alarmist reaction based on *fact* or a pessimistic view of how people would behave in an environment free of Management interference? Is it based on a supposition that armies of people would stare into space, not understanding or willing to carry out tasks and service they have done for years? Wouldn't Employees spend all day gazing out of the window to no good effect at all? Or, is it a more alarming (and perhaps true) recognition that the work, effort, toil and sweat of creating an organisational structure is a fruitless and unnecessary exercise? Certainly it would be the case if every Manager *was* indeed absent and the factory, office and institution carried on regardless.

When Managers are absent – either on a course, or an 'away-day'- the fact is that everything carries on as normal. The plan is produced and broadly followed, phones are answered, the production lines keep running, the orders are packed and invoices are sent out. There is nothing untoward and the apparatus still keeps revolving. There are some differences: some of the noise is removed, the flapping, the urgency and the interference whilst at the same time, the changes in direction evaporate and everything ticks along like a regular timepiece.

There should be no great disappointment that this is the case. It is the result of Employees' ability to organise themselves with the skills and wherewithal accumulated over days, weeks, months and years. It is symptomatic of human's nature capacity to adapt and learn and to appreciate a situation in which they evidently know their jobs without outside interference. There is a collective appreciation that work has to be done, that there are pressures and deadlines known to most and appreciated by everyone. Managers should not fear being absent. They should not recoil at their dispensability, they should embrace it.

However, it has become a persuasive absolute and article of faith that organisations cannot function without Management. If it was true, it would be disingenuous of me to stipulate the opposite. It would also be hypocritical to blithely proceed with the subject of Management without asking a blunt question: if the great battalions of Management did not exist before, why is it now a requirement and what is its purpose? It is too simplistic to argue they are a by-product of the post-industrial era. The instruction manual for a Spinning Jenny did not have on its cover: 'For the express attention of the Manager in charge'; that the success of the military hierarchy was copied to the battlefields of commerce; that the flood of labour from the fields heralded the need for Captains, Sergeants and Corporals to tell them what was required; that the advent of ever more complicated processes could not work without a person in authority. Surely the answer must be that the whole operation would grind to a halt if 'Management' was not present. Surely, the requirement is to keep things ticking along, to make sure people are doing their jobs - and doing those properly?

The question is whether this is the desired outcome? It is easy to come to the opinion that there is an engineered reality used as evidence to prove that an army of Managers is vital for the success of any business or public institution. A rationale has been built that creates a vast game, pieced together with people's careers at stake - where ambitions and aspirations can be fulfilled in a rush to make money and exert huge amounts of influence and power. It is not difficult to see why this could be considered self-serving – creating an expansive theme park filled with toys, tools, methods and techniques, an array of assorted switches, lever and pulleys that determine not only how the game is played but how successful it will be for each participant. Equally challenging is the question regarding the exclusivity of these tools and methods. 'Engagement', 'Quality Circles' and 'Involvement' are only perceived as additional tricks and devices rather than an established goal. Communication skills and techniques are an imperative but only so long as they establish the organisation in the same mould and use the same paradigms of old. Management training and personal development are only for those of established rank and seniority; principles of improvement are only given to those who could possibly understand.

The finest plans are always ruined by the littleness of those who ought to carry them out, for the Emperors can actually do nothing. Bertolt Brecht

The trouble is, the role of the Manager has become synonymous with the delusion of indispensability. The Management class has grown exponentially over the last one hundred years so that every organisation, every enterprise, every Company has some form of hierarchy - however disjointed and insular. Rather than focusing on skilled artisans and practitioners, an army of administrators has grown to govern the machinery of the business: to make improvements, to make the process more efficient and to maximise profitability. If people get in the way, (which they invariably do) then the writing is on the wall. The 'organisation chart' crammed with the rectangular boxes of middle Management *is* the Company. The organisation chart *is* the manifestation of how the Company operates and the key people within it even though Employees on the shopfloor struggle to get a mention. Those actually doing the work appear as a number or an anonymous box representing a department or a category of worker, permanent, part-time or agency staff. Before starting any work in any Company, I religiously ask for an organisation chart. The important personalities appear in a regimented structure that epitomises the executive integrity of the business they run. Not only does it create the fabric and perceived solidity within a Company, it becomes the direct focus of attention for armies of consultants, suppliers, training institutions, seminars, pedlars and charlatans.

The questions, in all their glaring consequence, are: do we need Managers? Do we need bureaucrats? Do we need administrators? Should we not rely on our inherent human instinct that wills us to cooperate, innovate and organise? Or do we need leaders, visionaries and creative souls who can nurture and inspire groups and individuals with energy, creativity and verve?

Definitions are never exact...

In an advertisement for a school of Leadership Techniques, the discipline or skill of Management was described as the ability to "manipulate people into doing things that you need to get done". I read twice, just to make sure. Ask most people about the role of Management and most would say: the business of 'getting people to do things'. The definition in the dictionary states that Management is: *"The process of dealing with or controlling things or people"* and uses as an example: *"the Management of deer"*. The last example gives the game away (no pun intended). Other definitions state it is the act of 'organising' or 'coordinating' - or any other synonym - to achieve certain goals and ambitions. A fuller definition uses words such as 'leading', 'planning' and 'controlling' – in fact, all the words that imply authority and superiority using language that conveys the marshalling of resources to meet particular needs. It carries the loud ring of militarism and still echoes the sentiments and objectives of *Sun Tzu*.

Is the problem caused by the role not being fully understood? Is it because, by its very nature, Management is a shifting target, a multi-faceted profession that has very few common denominators? If the Manager needs to practice like a musician, what do they need to practice? If the definition is misconstrued and wrong, then the targeted training and practice is also likely to be wide of the mark. Like sending someone to practice on a tuba before learning the violin, the lesson might be informative but ultimately impractical.

The Current Conundrum

A Starting Point

If I am questioning the accepted role of a Manager, am I not also undermining my own basis for writing this book? Isn't this all going to be self-defeating and contradictory? I am sure that the years spent as a Management Consultant leaves me open to all sorts of accusations and an instinctive reaction: who am I to write about an established profession – and by doing so, question its very existence? Who am I to query the role of the Manager, what a Manager should do and whether Managers are requirements for a successful business or not? Well, with no other premise that it has been *my* profession and *my* job for over a quarter of a century. I have been through the mill as much, if not more, than anyone else - which doesn't give me a medal, just a wider canvas to paint a picture of contemporary Management practices. Even more importantly, I have spent a career making the same mistakes as everyone else. I would argue that I could only be open to the charge of hypocrisy and the undermining of my own position if I was to agree that the job of 'Management' – the job as it is carried out now – is the right one. If my reasoning contained the axiom: 'Carry on doing what you are doing, just do it better!' my argument would be redundant and superfluous.

But here is the problem. Working within organisations, the largest portion of my time is spent with Managers and Leaders, instilling, amongst other things, organisational skills, the effective allocation of time and resource, designing meeting structures and ensuring that information systems serve their purpose. In most cases, all these improvement are not strictly intrinsic to the Process but form the peripheral elements deemed useful in getting the work done *properly*. Isn't this bizarre? Isn't this a strange set of circumstances? Why should so much time be spent on organising the people whose job it is to organise? Why is there so much effort spent on training people who should be carrying out the training? Why is so much money and effort needed to convince those in charge to communicate with the very people with whom they are employed to communicate? Why am I supposed to be adding value within any business for the very people whose sole purpose it is to do the same? In what other profession would these anomalies be found?

In every business, in ever organisation, I hear complaints about people who are not motivated, of people who are not organised, of those who are not engaged or involved. This is all very well, except there is a deep absurdity in the fact that these complaints are from the very people tasked with motivating, organising, engaging and involving those who are complaining. The irony is palpable. I have had to train Managers to motivate the people who, by their very actions, they have de-motivated; programmes to get Managers to empower groups of people, that by their deeds they have disenfranchised; expend enormous efforts to organise Employees with those whose job it is to coordinate and utilise; there are coaching sessions, about coaching, given to the very people who are hired to coach. Managers have to be *persuaded* to challenge people and the organisation, which was the sole purpose and reason for their employment in the first place. There is precious little time spent with those who are doing the work and not enough incentive to do so. The conflict is exacerbated when Managers have to spend time with consultants, advisors and colleagues and directors, resulting in ever decreasing amounts of time spent with those on the production lines, desks, machines and work-benches that are ultimately providing the services for which the Company is wholly dependent.

If men are to respect each other for what they are, they must cease to respect each other for what they own. A.J.P. Taylor

I know this is heresy – and in my chosen profession, perilous. But to shy away from this central point would be dishonest and duplicitous. We are not talking about those on probation, in an apprenticeship, under 'supervision' or undergoing a prolonged, institutional audition. 'They', 'we', 'us' are all fully paid cornerstones in a construction of hierarchy, with an overriding ambition to make a sizeable profit margin - *the means by which are either abandoned or institutionally under-utilised.*

Given this paradox, would it not be pertinent to ask what drives and engages Employees? Are they inspired and empowered or are they becoming increasingly demoralised by the interference of Management levels, who perhaps have no interest and knowledge of those providing them with their income and status? The question is significant, appropriate and given free rein, could well be morally depressing. For anyone with a truly objective and rational viewpoint the whole arrangement of organisational hierarchies as they currently work, is bewildering and nonsensical.

There is a more deep-seated moral dilemma. Managers have within their grasp the lives and livelihoods of people who rely on their abilities, influence and integrity. The well-being, security and *happiness* of Employees can be changed on a whim. So, a Manager's competence to do the job in hand becomes even more critical and leads to some very awkward questions. When we entrust a Manager or a Supervisor with a group of people, what would happen if they asked for his or her qualifications? 'You have in your charge, my well-being, my safety, my effectiveness, my contribution, my ambition, my job security, my mortgage, my rent, my children, my partner and our livelihoods in your hands. What qualifies you to be in that position?' There would be an uncomfortable splutter and an arrogant reproach. 'How dare you?' the Manager would say. 'How dare *you*!' might well be the riposte

The Problem Compounded

This provides some background to the absurdity of Employees who are quickly and regularly criticised for *not* being motivated, organised, involved and more efficient –by the very people whose job it is to make sure they can be. The people, the culture and the environment all get the blame - all the things that need to be shaped and changed by a Manager to create a better working environment. There are those Managers who don't see the problem at all; there are those with a look of bewilderment and exasperation etched on their faces; there are others who realise that something has to change. The question is, where does the responsibility and accountability lie?

"Get in at the deep end – it's the only way to learn", "Sink or swim", "Try and stay afloat and you will be okay". Every aquatic metaphor known to man is thrown at the newly appointed Manager as though they are to undergo some primitive form of initiation ceremony. A few chosen ones acknowledge defeat very early on. Most, struggle on. Some are able to keep their heads above water, but only just. Of course, part of this predicament, stems from the fact that some are in the wrong job. If the truth be told, it is not easy for anyone to refuse promotion, advancement and recognition and the first step on a career path to executive stardom. Very few feel confident enough to say, "No" to a higher income and increased authority. It is extremely difficult given this predicament to make an unemotional decision of whether they are capable of taking on the mantle of Management. At times, the aspiring leader rises through the pecking order and the range of training, development plans, coaching and mentoring programmes become more available. A surfeit of opportunities are presented and taken and the *completion* box is conveniently 'ticked'. Time Management is a problem? Let's do a course on that! People not feeling part of the organisation? Let's give Management a course on coaching! Rules not being applied, unruly staff, lack of discipline? Let's send those supervisors on a 'Conflict Management' course!

If a problem is too difficult to solve, one cannot claim that it is solved by pointing at all the efforts to solve it. Hannes Alfven

The much quoted 'Peter Principle' is still as relevant today as when it was first published in 1969. Employees get promoted to a level above their existing capabilities. The principle is clearly exemplified when the most productive line-operators are promoted to the ranks of Management on the solitary basis that they are the best at what they do. The organisation inherits a poor Manager and loses their best operator. It serves a number of purposes: the gap is filled in the supervisory vacancy, with a person who knows the ropes, an experienced 'technician' who has been taught the tricks of the trade and, just as importantly, someone who is supposed to be beholden and grateful. And why shouldn't they be? When entrusted with responsibility and authority, people's natural defences inhibit asking relevant questions that sow the seeds of doubt with those that have placed them there. It becomes an impertinence to question the wisdom of their decision. People tend to get on with it. That is not to say that the new Manager is happy; that is not to say that the people on the Shopfloor are ecstatic about 'one of their own' becoming 'one of them'. It is not to say that Employees and colleagues alike see it as fair and deserved.

People are still promoted for the wrong reasons in unfavourable circumstances. In most other professions, handing over a level of authority to anyone with little training, little or no experience, little support and an unknown aptitude would not be considered. 'Knowing the area', 'knowing the department' and 'knowing the product' is not enough – and never will be. I have met many who are placed in positions of authority and responsibility with little or no preparation and whilst many are unqualified, some are unsuitable and unfortunately, should not be there at all. Nevertheless, the Peter Principle is not just about promoting people above their competence. That is not the point. No, we tend to promote people above their *present* ability –not necessarily their potential.

A Question of Status

Our love of our work is consistent with what it provides. Work furnishes a need of the intellect, of status, salary, perks and authority. We aspire to be the person who can sign a piece of paper from which a myriad of decisions are made, equipment purchased and contracts sealed and delivered. It becomes easy to take on the mantle of 'arbiter' and 'oracle'. The person who has the authority to hire and fire; the one who can sanction a bonus, perks, rewards; the one who can put the fear of god into people with all sorts of assumed punishments; the one who can grant promotion as quickly as they can assign the worst conceivable tasks; the one who decides, the judge and the jury, the person of power with *right* on their side.

It is a compulsive task, a position with great obligations, tremendous weight and truly life-changing authority. The trouble is that being 'up to your neck' is one thing - struggling with a sea of contentious people and daily dilemmas come with their own set of challenges. Disputes need the Wisdom of Solomon and rewards need to gratify the one and satisfy the many.

Status and authority are reinforced by behaviour and the trappings of office. If the Manager's role is ever brought into question, there are tangible pieces of evidence that Managers can use: I have a Company car; I have a reserved parking spot; I get a bonus; I am allowed to come and go as I please; I am busier than others; I am under more pressure; I suffer more stress; my phone is always switched on; I have meetings to attend and I have decisions to make!

By working faithfully eight hours a day, you may eventually get to be a boss and work twelve hours a day. Robert Frost

It becomes easy for certain assumptions to be made. It becomes a trap in which we can easily fall – a consequence of the environment and a modest dose of self-belief. It is a deception made of assumptions - those assumptions being that the Manager is more astute, wiser, and adept than the person reporting to them. It is an assumed intelligence, a presumed authority and imagined wisdom. Very rarely is it questioned. At times the Manager may encounter a continuous battle with those articulate, reasoned and anarchistic enough to challenge them. Most often, the Manager can lay waste to any objections as subordinates have to bow to organisational authority. Irrespective, it is more often than not seen as a battlefield when it should be quite the opposite.

The reality is that people just have different jobs to do. It is hardly fair to accuse people of not understanding, not knowing what is going on, not realising the importance of good customer service, not understanding costs especially when they are not told, when they are not involved or when it is a 'secret'. I am not suggesting that people have the same aspirations, dreams, ambitions, acumen or skills to reach the same level of understanding and competency. I just think it is wrong to assume that they don't! It becomes a starting point before any word is exchanged, before any opinion is spoken and before any interest has been shared. Everyone has potential, from the man on the shopfloor to the CEO. The trouble is that training and development is not given to the Shopfloor operator before they are promoted and the CEO believes that no one is qualified to give them any training at all. The problem is therefore, that the man on the shopfloor is unaware - or has not been given the opportunity to reach their potential - and the senior person believes they have reached theirs!

This perception of status is not in the least helpful and does no-one any good. The Operator on the shopfloor is just as likely to be as skilled and adept at doing what he or she does and is probably no less talented or intelligent than the young Manager who has an MBA. They are just good at different things. It is a matter of perspective and circumstance. The skilled person may not have the requisite training to fulfil the role of Manager just as the Manager would not have the experience or training to fulfil the demands required of an Operator. Responsibilities and levels in the hierarchy get confused with intelligence and insight. Humility is in short supply, regardless of how the word is construed. It is not the language of the meek, the terminology of the defeated nor the words of the humble. It is an acknowledgement that status and salary are not necessarily transmitters of great understanding and knowledge. Unless there has been some intense overnight reading, the Manager promoted from being an Operator the day before has roughly the same amount of insight and awareness the day after. Unfortunately and inevitably, the sensitivities and expectations change - and the gameplay and rules are altered accordingly.

"I must be a great Boss, no one likes me."

Sometimes the façade crumbles and in the heat of any dispute, the Manager has to say: "I am your Boss!" It is a dispiriting and discomforting outburst. There are no winners. Having to shout this out to those who have obviously failed to comprehend the organisational imperative has the ring of desperation, the chime of defeat and the crying appeal for some respect. It destroys the proposition by its very utterance.

In a recent study on Management and success, one conclusion was that, whereas *respect* and *fairness* were required attributes, being *liked* was not. In fact, the report went on to say that those people who are '*liked*' or '*liked to be liked*' are usually consigned to the darkest corners of the office, hidden away with their careers coming to an ignominious halt. The inference is that you have to be a 'go-getter', a maverick of sorts, willing to achieve ambitions and goals regardless (and in spite of) the people with whom you work. Success is achieved by those who can ride slip-shod across other's careers; by those who have clear and coherent goals very much like the worst candidates in the 'The Apprentice', whose singularity of purpose and complete antipathy for others is only equalled by their candid streak of stupidity. The *will* to succeed becomes confused with *being* successful.

The question is, does a Manager gauge his or her success on their own achievements or by the success of those people they are supposed to be managing? Can a Manager really be seen as effective if the people under them are constantly under-achieving? Well, 'yes', apparently (and unfortunately) you can, especially if you subscribe to the traditional mantra: 'you can only deal with the people you are given' which is never mentioned as an aspirational challenge but as a statement of fact and by implication, unalterable. It is too easy and too convenient to assume the mantle of a 'victim'. In doing so, the only way to gain success is to get rid of those who do not shine - or to pass them on to any another unwitting colleague.

We like to be liked and we like to be respected; we like recognition and we like affirmation. There are, of course, those who say they do not care whether they are liked or not – but there are fewer who actually believe it. Often, the words: "I don't care what they think!" is the first reaction to rebellion and resistance for any new idea but this bellicose belligerence is entirely fabricated and has more to do with stubbornness and implied righteousness than a conviction that popularity is negligible and superfluous. However much we agree with the conclusions of surveys and regardless of the extent to which we would like to embrace the notion of a loner, we are too much of a social animal. This lends itself to another dilemma: if people like to be respected why don't we, as a matter of course, adopt the behaviours that will promote the desired response? Why do our actions conflict with our nature?

There is an inherent contradiction in the way we want success – the way we want to achieve greatness – and our natural instincts and our knowledge of what works and what doesn't. There is an internal, psychological rebellion – a counter-intuitive response to the situation in which we find ourselves. We get angry, we get frustrated, we want people to do things the way we would like them to be done but we do not always act in a way that will promote the best response.

So long as men worship the Caesars and Napoleons, Caesars and Napoleons will duly arise and make them miserable. Aldous Huxley

Why is this? Is it because we are all conflicted individuals or that we are all psychologically mis-wired pretenders? Or is it that the signals, the commands, the role-models we inherit, the instructions, lessons and survey conclusions lead us in one direction whilst our own personality leads us in quite another? Is it because the models of success are painted and adorned with traits that are superficial and misleading? Or is that it becomes too becomes difficult to believe that the poor soul who is painted as a self-centred mogul is also possessed of the same frailties, longings and insecurities as the rest of us? There is a common perception that there are 'leaders' and 'followers' in this world – a regimented pre-selection of the population with two essential characteristics. The fleeting observation that one may be a 'follower' leads to all sorts of behaviours that try to prove the opposite whilst the 'leader' tries to balance the requisite empathy with the trappings of self-entitlement and arrogance. Both are distasteful. Yet, all leaders start as 'followers' and many 'followers', given the right aspirational qualities and conditions, are perfectly able to 'lead'. It is never black and white.

The road to leadership is a well-worn path of ambition, determination, hard work, experience, circumstance, talent and fortune. The pre-requisites of a 'great leader', somewhat mistakenly, become a suite of behavioural characteristics that are incongruous and misunderstood. It is like getting to the front of the queue where sharp elbows, precociousness and the inconsideration of others seems to be the ultimate way of getting ahead. The phrase, 'be careful how you treat people on the way up as you might have to meet them again on the way down', betrays a number of stereotypes: that firstly, it is accepted practice to 'do the dirty' on people on the way up and that being at the top is only temporary.

And yet...whenever I ask a group of Managers the question: "Name your favourite boss and describe their characteristics", without fail, there are references to Leaders, Managers, Mentors and Coaches that exude traits far removed from the archetypal maverick and managerial 'climber'. They describe people who were (or are) good 'listeners', good 'encouragers', people who accepted mistakes – even expected mistakes to be made - people who were empathetic and though they not always sought respect, were likely to respect others. They were inclusive, informative, they were kind and caring but most of all, they always had time for the person in question; a boss who worked tirelessly for their benefit; one who was focused on creating the conditions for their success and on their terms; someone who believed in their potential and where no effort was spared. I have known people to mention their own Father as their best 'boss' -the one who trusted them, the one who inspired them, who congratulated their strengths and forgave them their weaknesses. There is a persistent, common thread: one of enduring patience, of energy, of consistent, supportive behaviour and of always sparing the time. No one mentions the Managers who only had their own ambitions in mind; no one mentions the disgruntled, moody prima-donnas who see their staff as stepping stones to pasture new; no one follows a leader, or has respect for a Manager, if they are lazy and absorbed in how they appear to others. Having to 'clear up the mess' after someone who is neither diligent, meticulous, resourceful nor interested, regardless of how inherently qualified they are, is off-putting and unendurable. The political animals are usually best left to their own devices.

This might all sound understandable – even self-evident. And yet... the question is always posed just minutes *after* asking a more direct question: "What are the attributes of a successful Manager?" Here the response is strikingly different: you must be 'ambitious', 'smart', 'political' and 'quick-witted', you must be one who gets (and demands) 'respect', is 'firm but fair', 'incisive' and, in terms of any consensual, behavioural continuum, quite 'authoritarian'.

Everyone involved in this exercise is surprised by the contradiction – not just because it had not been considered - but in the light of the glaring anomaly of what is believed to be 'good' and what is *experienced* as 'good'. There is a clear and distinct dichotomy between experience and perception. It is obvious but contradictory; it is rational but puzzling; self-evident but absurd. It becomes like two opposing aspirations: there is understanding what I *know* I should do and what I *believed* I should do. There is a clear divide between the pursuit of one's own success in deference to making every effort to ensure the success of others.

This exercise illuminates a number of frustrations and contradictions and explains why many are not the Managers they believe they should be. For many there is an implied imperative to be firm and to demand respect -

but it is unfamiliar territory. Traditionally, when we think of how to be a great Manager, a great 'Boss', we think we have to be more ruthless, more 'decisive' more political, more opportunistic, manipulative and autocratic. It is the result of the constant drumming and propaganda that is promulgated to make the Manager - as well as everyone else - more efficient, more driven, more focused and ultimately more successful. Be assertive! Be ruthless! Get results whatever the cost! Sharpen those elbows and use them! The aim of being a successful Manager becomes a façade of authoritarianism and a role best played by a qualified actor; a game to be played with the need for prompts and idiot boards around the office as reminders to be aloof, selfish and ambitious!

Don't get me wrong, there are people out there for whom playing a tyrant is second nature; there are those who have a shard of ice as their soul and who make you wonder whether heart donors can survive long after the operation. There are others with so little self-esteem and so little confidence, the only weapons at their disposal are fear and intimidation. Additionally, there are autocratic leaders who leave a road filled with the debris of human disappointment and bewilderment. They are, thankfully, the minority – the ones who stick out, either through their own pugnaciousness or ambitions of infamy.

However much the path lies between the two methods; however much we have to veer from one side to the other, whilst striving to be a strong leader, it is quite easy to forget how to become a great boss. So, where would you rank? Given the same exercise, what would people say about you? Would you mind? Does your ideal match your ambitions? Have you ever been mentioned as someone's 'Best Boss'?

We have to ask ourselves these questions in light of what we want to achieve and what makes us most successful. We have to be extremely honest when we ask ourselves, what makes a good leader? Does it contain this more deeply entrenched humanistic aspect? Or does it contain the more clinical aspects of providing strong direction, providing a vision, a mission and a clear strategy? Shouldn't we also include *compassion*, *honesty*, *respect*, *integrity*, *wisdom*, *fairness*, a good ear and a good heart? There is a recognised contrast between strength and apparent 'softness'. Here lies the struggle; here lies the challenge. More importantly, there is another way of looking at this – to add some perspective and to shift the direction one can take: a Manager should embrace work not just because of what it gives them but what it gives others.

Everyone has their own style

It is widely accepted that a great Leader is able to provide a clear strategy and direction. It is also accepted that a good Manager is able to take that strategy and direction and, regardless of its quality, translate it into specific activities within the organisation and ensure that they are done. There is nothing wrong with this except in the way the strategy is defined, interpreted, communicated and ultimately implemented. It is but a short leap to suggest that a Manager's sole purpose is to get things done through other people. I do not discount for one minute that there are many who might say: 'Yes, that's exactly what I want to do!' to 'I want to get people to specifically do the things I believe need to be done' and, 'Not only as *I* want done but what my *boss* wants done'. And his boss too!' Because, let's face it, my Boss knows what needs to happen, he knows the 'end-goal', we just have to get on with it!'

Is this a distorted view of responsibilities? Is this a true reflection of what happens in most organisations? The wave of instructions stream down the sides of the pyramid and splash into the organisation in a way that is disparate and chaotic. And whilst reluctantly accepting this state of affairs, it becomes more than difficult to keep people in line with a common thread, with a common set of values and an agreed strategy. It means that Managers have to be malleable and adopt different styles that work - styles that convey a message and ultimately will get the job done. Each Manager has his or her own style and it becomes a natural precondition to suit the circumstances, the environment, the people that have to be 'dealt with' and the culture they inhabit.

The pursuance of labels and Management styles is a narrow, pigeon-holing of general characteristics that lend themselves to generalist conditions. To fabricate a concise framework in which to utilise a particular style of engagement lends itself wonderfully to the shopping-market shelves of human understanding. It is a convenience which is both distorted and misrepresentative. It becomes a *style* 'to manipulate people into doing things that need to be done'. The words, 'trick' and 'subterfuge' come to mind as though Employees are a willing and gullible audience ready to be duped by the latest play on words, pseudo-science, Management-Speak and labelling. Choosing the right type of style greatly impacts how Employees work and how they respond. It becomes a pragmatic curve – a vital set of behaviours that shadow the best of intentions and cloud the worst of decisions.

The behaviour of any bureaucratic organization can best be understood by assuming that it is controlled by a secret cabal of its enemies. ― Robert Conquest.

In my founding years as a Management Trainer I was as culpable as anyone else. 'Management Styles' and their usage was a *must* for any aspiring Manager and a requisite part of the syllabus. It was taught that any Manager – a successful and 'complete' Manager –needed to adopt a certain style based on current circumstances and the Manager's purpose. In other words, what the Manager wanted to 'get out of' the situation.

It is an unhappy irony that teachers become the chief

perpetrators of some of the worst afflictions. 'Management Styles' sound as though they are taken from a pre-feudal, military context and hark back to an age when subjugates had to be ruled, rather than motivated; a time when Employees had to be controlled rather than inspired. Even so, styles nowadays have become a touch more enlightened and sophisticated:

- Autocratic Leadership – *apparently, this is the most efficient but is rarely engaging. It is the short-cut to getting a message across without undue explanation.*
- Bureaucratic Leadership – *is, by all accounts, best in environments where Employees need to follow the rules - which pre-supposes that people don't normally follow them and need brow-beating by a faceless official.*
- Charismatic Leadership – *is the nod to the power of the personality and is open to all graduates from charm school. It is where the cult of the individual has its church, which often leads to the perception of self-importance and delusions of grandeur.*
- Democratic/Participative Leadership – *is a consensus style of Management which is described as a slow course of action but is a step forward in terms of engagement.*
- Laissez-Faire Leadership – *is a method of letting people 'get on with it' which is fine if people are sufficiently skilled, aware and astute but is often attributed to a lack of energy rather than an determined philosophy.*
- People-Oriented/Relations-Oriented Leadership – *which can lead to good team work and cooperation but is often*

dependent on the volatility and longevity of the relationship, especially when things become chaotic.
- Servant Leadership – *giving people the lead which can foster high morale but can be confused with giving people everything they <u>feel</u> they need.*
- Task-Oriented Leadership *which is an iron-clad, General Patton style of getting the job done!*
- Transactional Leadership – *which is a practice of 'Management by barter', a conducive and consensual 'back scratching' which translates to obeying the leader, clarifying roles and responsibilities and getting something in return.*
- Transformational Leadership – *which is touted as the best in most business situations.*

Management styles are still being taught as a method of self-enlightenment and the pathway to success. This misunderstanding, both of human nature and the role of the Manager is an unsophisticated and clumsy method of dealing with immediate situations that need resolution. By their very nature, they are all 'manipulative'. *'Avoiding the situation', 'blaming others', 'feigning ignorance'* are inelegant emotional tricks just as much as putting the 'fear of god' into people. These styles mark a distance – a Managerial gap in understanding: "I want something from you therefore I need to act in a particular way". The required response might be acquiescence, silence, acceptance or cooperation - but they are all temporary. When a new situation occurs, a new style has to be selected from the jukebox of Management performances. Adopting a style for a particular set of circumstances covers a multitude of sins and regardless of the situation requires a 'u - turn' not long afterwards.

Obviously, if the job is to 'get other people to *do* things', then certainly, some tricks, levers and other assorted mechanisms are needed to make it all work. In other words: "This is the predicament and this is how to get things done, regardless". It is a convenient and pragmatic approach to a myriad of potential problems, issues and conflicts all of which are generated by the one obstacle with which a Manager has to contend: people! Whether it be facile, immoral or wide of the mark, Management Styles illuminate a path, like landing lights for a wayward pilot. Suitable mannerisms, directives and modus operandi can, at some point, all be labelled and judged but recognised 'Styles' are banded about like remedies to curable but misjudged situations. Like the expediency of a late-night Chemist: "Take these tablets and you'll be right as rain", disregarding the causes and symptoms, influences and effects, either through little interest or little time.

The significance lies not in the question of style but the substance of the conversation. It is the relationship and the collaboration with people in the organisation that is the issue; it is the structured assistance and combined ambition; it is the *level* of cooperation and the struggle to meet organisational and individual objectives. To say that in a manufacturing environment, you need to adopt a more bureaucratic style of Management to make sure people follow the rules, is both crass and ultimately self-defeating; to demand the adoption of a democratic style in an open office environment is at once patronising and calculating.

I am quite sure there is a suitable label for every Manager we know. They may well fall into any one of the categories listed - even with an acknowledgement that people exhibit different behaviours given different situations. However, the point of this exercise cannot be to label other Managers. It is like labelling other drivers on the road without thinking of the way *you* need to drive and the direction *you* need to take. There are always pragmatic necessities given a constantly variable situation. The rational and logical shift from heart to the head is accelerated by the immediate conditions – and so it should be. It is no good practicing relationship Management and gaining democratic affiliation in a situation that requires immediate cost-cutting for the business to survive. This would be pushing the barriers of engagement and involvement to the limit. Kindness and empathy cannot be the reason a business has to shut its doors; failure to strip out costs exposing even more Employees to the queue of job-seekers cannot be in the interests of the greater good. Both are more akin to *avoidance* and is the cruel consequence failing to face facts and at the same time, not having the assurance to confront the immediate issues. By engaging with people, no one is necessarily bound to the old litany of using particular Management Styles to get what is 'needed' from people. This will always be symptomatic of a misguided mission to get people to do the things they would rather not do in the first place.

"There's nowt stranger than folk..."

Whether we fully agree with Maslow's 'hierarchy of needs' – and especially their respective ranking - there are fundamentals that need to be satisfied. Although Maslow did not actually draw a pyramid, it is a simple interpretation of how people prioritise basic and crucial needs. Human characteristics are not just shaped by environment and conscious or unconscious needs but on the aspirations of the community, the self, the organisational structure and the surrounding aspirational culture. The immediacy of those needs are determined by the context and by the immediate imperatives which, of course, can shift through any given period – not only for the individual in question but also for their peers.

In keeping with the processes and systems that are created, it is in our nature to be complicated and to complicate the environment we inhabit. The fervour by which academics like to group people into layers, hierarchies and social groupings leads not only to the simplification of the problem but also the simplification of any proposed answer. The importance is not in defining a structurally uniform set of values but in defining a set of needs which are distinct and understood by the individual and the group in which they co-exist. There may be a hierarchy of needs but there is also a hierarchy of ambitions, a hierarchy of potential and just as importantly, a hierarchy of beliefs. It is this segregation that makes people so interesting, so arresting and so challenging. We should appreciate this complication; we should recognise its value; we should appreciate its potential. So, why do we allow so many to feel unappreciated, under-valued and disrespected? Shouldn't it be the case that they are fundamental foundations for any organisation to succeed and principles to which any Employee can cling and trust?

A colleague of mine was in conversation outside a factory. 'How many work there?' he was asked. 'About half of them', he replied. Whether we like it or not, there is an unspoken acceptance that in every Company and every industry, we are only capable of utilising significantly less than the full potential of every Employee. There is common acknowledgement that many Employees, after clocking off, slip the shackles of employment and take on different personas: the accountant for their local club; the chairperson for their local committee; the spokesman for a lobby group; the referee, the artist, the writer, the musician. We know there is a reservoir of talent waiting to be given free rein and waiting for some acknowledgment and recognition. For while we may be aware that people have different talents and different strands of intelligence, there are a number of substantial obstacles: the perception by the majority that their position in the Company reflects the position they have in life, together with an unease that there could be hidden depths that would be potentially challenging and dangerous and that to liberate those talents could involve a lot of digging, soul-searching and effort. So much effort in fact that it may well detract from what we thought Management was all about – status, power, responsibility, authority, intellectual capability, material wealth and economic security.

There are many wonderful things and nothing is more wonderful than man. Sophocles

It is not an easy proposition and not one that can be addressed with a number of easy fixes. A number of conversations and briefings are not the only remedies that will send productivity and profitability soaring to unparalleled heights. This entrenched seam of energy does not come freely, it does not readily appear of its own and it requires planning, structured intervention, and skilled execution. But, for any Manager to cast doubt on the potential in other people is to cast doubt on their own abilities as a Manager. A Manager who does not believe in the potential of any individual casts a light on their own failings – and places a mirror on their own inadequacies.

Talking to a group of supervisors, one of them boldly

stated that: "You are only as good as the people below you". However ill-conceived, the perception still exists that Manager are victims of the quality of people they find under their supervision. The truth is that Supervisors and Managers are as good as the level of people they raise them to be. The reality is that they are only as *great* as the people for which they are responsible.

I am not preaching any great form of morality here – even though there is a clear moral dimension to a Manager's role. I am not arguing for the inherent "goodness" or even less that people will always excel. However, there is a fairly pragmatic and viable avenue for any business to pursue. It is an approach based on experience and observation that people are naturally gifted and talented however well-hidden and secretive this may appear. This should *not* be surprising to anyone and yet, unfortunately, it always *is* - a surprise that has an impact and consequence on the values and morality of the business and can, inevitably, inhibit a Manager's own success and potential achievement.

The Task in Hand...Getting better!

Throughout these pages, I will try to explore and extrapolate this notion - this compelling idea that the individuality, sporadic purpose, divergent ambitions and random nature of people is the true driving force that is often overlooked and smothered by archaic but pervasive Management practice; a situation that stifles the potential strength within any organisation. And if this is true – as most would have to admit – there has to be a change in the way that a Manager typically acts out *his* or *her* role. This is not to say this is a hidden gem upon which no one has yet stumbled. The question is: how much effort and energy has been expended in tapping the latent talent, creativity and ingenuity within each Employee within each organisation? This is the challenge and this is the job, regardless of how others like to conceal it with science, labels, new fads and technicalities.

He that is not aware of his ignorance, will be only misled by his knowledge. Richard Whately

There is no crime in self-praise and accepting compliments from others but the true test is to examine what could have been done better. There is a world of difference in saying: 'I'm here!' to 'I'm getting there!' There is a difference between a platform and a rung of a ladder. Even for the most talented, this is a difficult acknowledgment to make. The most astute are always compromised by their desire to ensure that people understand their cleverness, not their failings. But the wisest know they have a mountain to climb and wisdom is nothing more than the application of experience, knowledge and understanding. From that experience, decisions can and need to be made. A Leader or a Manager's task (or life itself) is made up of decisions that have to be made at the most inconvenient times. It is this that makes the task of Management the most challenging; it is this that creates a Manager's value. Those who perform a quick side-step are those that avoid the most crucial aspect of their role. Circumventing the challenge, avoiding the conflict – and the opportunity - is conspicuous and illuminates the Manager's true worth and their efficacy within the role.

But where to start? The introduction was all about *them*, the *others*, *those* not performing, wasn't it? But where is *our* starting point? Where do I as an individual stand? It is an important question if not the *most* important question. The answer, quite simply, depends on our understanding of the role and responsibilities that are part and parcel of being an everyday Manager, Supervisor, Director or Leader – and how that role is carried out in practice.

To that end, there needs to be a pointer: a direction or a general heading. There has to be a simpler description of a Manager. Let's start with one that is unpretentious and uncomplicated: *A Manager, as his or her sole purpose, is required to create the conditions of success for all the people, resources and machinery for which they are held responsible. A Manager needs to create those conditions of success so that people can prosper; so that people can reach their potential; so that they feel they can contribute and by doing so, experience a sense of personal achievement.* To that end, there is an enormous role to play - just *not* the one being played at the moment!

There is none so blind as those who will not see. Anon

By agreeing to this definition there needs to be an assessment. Before embarking on any journey there needs to be a point of departure, a stake in the ground. Every journey has a beginning, a 'middle bit' - but not necessarily an end. It is not only essential and pertinent, it also colours our opinions along the way, defines the length of travel and equips us for the trek ahead. One question leads to another: Where should we be? Where do we want to get to? How are we going to get there? How do we know we have arrived? What do we do when we get there?

Everything in this day and age is described as a 'journey' - a word that has become an irritating cliché and appears to describe a rudderless passage whereby everyone else is pulling the strings and the willing victim suffers a myriad of events and circumstances that are supposed to shape and mature them. The journey described here, has to be different. This is more like an expedition and in this context becomes a voyage that relies on one's own ambitions, taking a firm grip of the wheel, having one's feet firmly on the accelerator and, if necessary, every available appendage on the brake.

This becomes an opportunity for reflection and a critical diagnosis. However, this is not an exercise in penance, but an imperative to exploring one's own potential. The ability to develop as an excellent Manager lies in the readiness and enthusiasm to be critical about yourself whilst still having the energy, perseverance and obstinacy to keep striving. In self-examination, the truth needs to be used as the propulsion to enable us being better at what we do. This is not a religious purge of the soul; this is not the beginning of a crusade but it should define a new beginning. In this case it is not unlike a GP's surgery where the two most pertinent questions are: "What condition am I in?" and "What tablets do I need to take?" From experience I know that the diagnosis can be difficult to acknowledge and the remedy can be a difficult pill to swallow. It is however, an acknowledgment that things are not as they should be and that the condition can be improved.

Managers, no matter how good (or bad) they may be, face an unconquerable dilemma – a dilemma that has its roots in the quest to get better, to improve and to be the best one can be. Management is about learning through mistakes. Show me a Manager who does not admit to making mistakes and I will show you someone with either no experience, someone less than honest or one who has lost their grip of reality. Management, in its purest sense, is an extreme endurance test of learning, errors and achievements - not necessarily in that order and not entirely balanced. Any person's experience is a tapestry of errors that have been made unconsciously or consciously. The application of decisions and the instinctive willingness to implement changes will always lead to mistakes. Equally, in a situation where no mistakes are being made at all, it is questionable whether anything is being done at all.

Let's be honest: what is worse than being at fault? Is it being found out? Is it the knowledge that you need to keep getting better? Or much worse, is it not *knowing* you might be at fault? It is often excusable to be a poor - or not particularly adept Manager - *as long as you are aware of it.* It is more than natural to make a mistake but the bigger mistake is not to realise that one has been made. To admit, firstly to yourself and then to others, an error of judgement, a bad decision and a mistaken strategy takes some nerve but it is ultimately a measure of strength not of weakness. If the mistake is not even registered, it is nigh on impossible to be in a position to repair the damage. However solid the foundations seem to be, the cracks will always appear.

The only thing that could be worse than a Manager failing to recognise their own mistakes is the one who fails to realise how bad they are and compounds this unhappy misconception by believing they are really quite good. Management is like playing a musical instrument – an enterprise steeped with every opportunity to create harmony and discord. The worst musicians are those who not only play the wrong notes but are unaware that the wrong notes are being played - the rest of the group have to play on, cringing as one jarring phrase follows another and a flurry of false note spill off the fret-board without the faintest apology. To make the problem worse, the more senior the Manager, the more difficult it is for them to hear the truth – or for them to hear what is being said. The act of saying: "You didn't play that very well!" is both uncomfortable and unwelcome – and for many of the messengers, fraught with dire consequences.

No, when the fight begins within himself, a man's worth something. Robert Browning

The most important part of any Management development is self-examination: self-awareness coupled with acute and sometimes, painful honesty. Any Manager has to be resolute. The perception of how we perform is usually a construct of our imaginations: of what has been communicated, how it was communicated, how articulate the message was and whether it was new and innovative. Our experiences are not always governed by what we know but what we think we know. They are ruled by a combination of fact and perception. Discussions with Managers frequently hinge on what was *said* and not always what was *understood*. A Manager's opinion of what was communicated can easily differ (by some distance) from the listener's understanding of what was heard. This is neither by design nor accident. The range of filters contained within our ears carry as many variables as an encryption process for bank security. Everyone's thought process has more than a modicum of conceit: "I know what I wanted to say, and I am sure I said it". Even the best sound-bites of wisdom that unexpectedly trip from our tongues, the most considered observations and the most articulate conclusion to an argument can be comprehended as excessive verbiage, pompous drivel or vacuous declarations of an arrogant mind. Obviously, it is not what we want to tell people that is important but what we would like them to understand. The Manager's role in the world is not how he or she acts but how those actions are understood. If we are to assess our own development based on our own personal evaluation, would this differ significantly from what the perception of others? More than likely. If we scored ourselves on sociability, effectiveness, impact, delivery and 'usefulness' to the organisation, would our results be different to those scored by others? Almost definitely. The point is, we are never our own best judges. The worst person to proof-read any document is the author; the worst person to appraise a piece of music is the composer. We are dismal at judging our own behaviour and are deliberately misleading when we talk about our own perception of events.

Mistakes are best concealed by those who make them. Admitting those mistakes can be both a humbling and an important discipline not only in the world of Management but also in an everyday social context. Everyone can be better at what they do; everyone can improve; everyone has not yet met their true potential. To overcome the barriers are the challenges in life, the biggest challenge is to take the road in the first place. This takes nerve and confidence.

Being confident - and having confidence in others - is an essential requirement for any successful Manager. A Manager has to believe in others as well as possessing sufficient self-belief. Even the best achievers suffer from the 'imposter syndrome' and attribute their success to luck, timing or the alignment of the stars. This crisis of confidence is shared by most Managers and Leaders and is best overcome by the recognition that it exists. Recognising a mistake, acknowledging fault and taking responsibility can be a clear indication of confidence: confidence in yourself but also in the organisation. Conversely, hiding mistakes and blaming others is a telling sign of a Manager's insecurity. Like fear, it leads to a tunnel-visioned view of the world. At best it is being uncertain of the repercussions of making an error and therefore minimising risk. It leads to concentrating on what is *known* and giving a wide berth to all that is *uncertain*.

"Don't tell me how bad it is Doctor."

Before starting any journey it is important to agree the point of departure: how far will you get preparing for a final assault on Everest when you are not even at Base Camp One? Equally, why be fully equipped for a long march when you only have to make a few strides? Why take all the detours given by others when the destination is just around the next corner? However obvious this point may be, think of this another way. Ask yourself, 'How good a Manager am I?' 'Where do I stand on the training curve?' 'How much do I still need to learn?' 'To what extent do people listen, respect or even like me?' 'Do I have a reputation of insight, wisdom, compassion and getting things done – or one that is completely the opposite?'

Nowadays, there are all types of surveys, questionnaires and various forms of tests to ascertain where people *are* in relation to one another. Personal profiles and '360°' feedback analyses ask people and colleagues what they think of you and others. By their very nature, they include what you would want to hear and what you especially *don't* want to hear. Yet, even the results are filtered and coloured by one's own interpretation and excused by status, understanding, motive and the mood of the day. People, given the right opportunity, are interested in where they are as long as it is not too distant from their own observations and does not acutely challenge their own sensitivities. Every test and survey result is digested to align with our own version of the *truth*.

Do they really give a good impression of how people rank as a Manager? It always becomes a test for the 'examiner' to see whether they have 'found them out' - a simple 'cat and mouse' where no one gets hurt. This is a strange set of affairs. Does this mean that the surveys never get it right or that it is a terrifying acknowledgement if one admitted they had got it 'spot on?' Why should we be hiding? What are we afraid of?

It is an inconvenient truth that men are never more insulted than when they hear the truth about themselves. Then again, sometimes we have to listen. Not just to the elements of a simple test or a generic psychometric analysis but to the world around us. Yes, *you* might be a great Manager but why are people not listening? Why do people not do as *you* ask? Why is it that people do not understand? Why are *your* ideas not granted the status they deserve? When you have an open door policy, why is there not a queue outside?

The trouble with most of us is that we would rather be ruined by praise than saved by criticism. Norman Vincent Peale

Even when opinion is asked for, the truth can rankle and hurt. The start of any cure starts with one simple principle: a recognition (and acknowledgement) that the situation can be improved. To set yourself free (by this, I mean embarking on the road to improvement) starts with a clear diagnosis and appreciation of where you stand – not just with regard to the guarded perceptions of your colleagues but through clinical and objective examination. It can be unpleasant because it will never answer one's own perceptions; it will never echo the shouts of greatness and it will never mirror the congratulatory exclamations of success. But it will be the best - no, it is the *only* starting point – and it can release so many from the shackles that keep them from their own potential.

This journey in this context is about *change* and *managing change*. Managing change is not just about each individual Manager but also the surrounding environment for which each Manager has responsibility. It is about creating the conditions for change and for success. That, in essence, *is* what Management is about. The starting point is not given by a set of answers but by a set of questions which only each Manager can or needs to answer.

Where do you stand?

In your role as a Manager, try and answer the following critically and honestly.

1. On a scale of 1-10 how do you rate yourself as a Manager where '1' is 'poor' and '10' is 'excellent'?
2. On a scale 1-10 how do you rate yourself in terms of being autocratic to consultative where '1' is very autocratic and 10 is consultative?
3. Are you in control?
4. Do you like people?
5. How much time do you spend speaking to the people for whom you have responsibility?
6. In total, what percentage of your day is spent with the members of your team?
7. What is it that motivates your people?
8. Do you pay Employees bonuses?

9. On what grounds are bonuses paid?
10. Do you consider yourself a Manager or a Leader?
11. Are you prone to let people 'get away with things' or do you confront issues immediately?
12. What changes have you made in your department recently?
13. To what extent were the people affected by the change involved in the process?
14. What recent changes have you made to your own routines and behaviours?
15. How effective are the meeting you attend?
16. How well do you organise your time?
17. Are you able to plan your day or are you subject to other's priorities?
18. How much work have you delegated today?
19. How much time in the day is spent on training other people?
20. How much time in the past year have you spent learning to be a better Manager?
21. How would you describe the Culture in the organisation?
22. What elements of that Culture do you feel you yourself have contributed?
23. What are the elements in that Culture that really hinder progress?
24. Are you a risk-taker or do you prefer caution?
25. Is there anyone you truly admire?
26. If so, what traits do they have that you would like to emulate?

27. If no one comes to mind, how do you shape your ambitions?
28. Are you a *good* boss or a *great* boss?
29. When was the last time someone said you are a *good* or a *great* boss?

So, how did you do? How did you mark yourself? To what extent were you hyper-critical and to what extent did you err on the side of congratulatory praise? If criticality is the first pre-requisite stage of improvement, then it can't be all bad whereas the veil of self-indulgence can be limiting and unrewarding. There is no definitive score but I hope to offer my view of current Management practice using each of these questions as a starting point.

As mentioned earlier, unless we are in a perfect place, unless our own diagnosis has revealed that we excel at everything, then, by definition, things have to *change*.

If you do not change direction, you may end up where you are heading. Lao Tzu

We can keep to what we know, with the things which we are comfortable, with the things that are considered less of a risk. The alternative is to set off on a new course with new objectives, new targets, new ambitions and a dusted down set of values. However, the haste to reach one's own chosen goals can be littered with a whole set of limitations and hindrances. Where each of us find ourselves in this context becomes vital in determining where we have to go and how long it will take.

No Manager is an island. By asking anyone to change, it is important to consider the elements that made them the way they are. Although a different direction can be proposed – a different set of values and behaviours – it is impossible to accomplish without taking the environment into the equation. There has to be a defined context and an examination of the structure and influences of the organisation into which each person is placed. By neglecting these all-important considerations, there are only two likely outcomes after any 'change' process – either the Manager will find somewhere else to exercise their talents or the conditions will revert to the way they were. So, not only do we need to describe those conditional elements, there has to be a structural and practical way of changing them, otherwise *everything* remains the same.

It would be disingenuous and condescending to cast aspersions on the current state of Management practice without offering a path to tread. Describing what is wrong – or the trouble with current Management practice – can only be done genuinely when a different avenue is suggested. Otherwise the hypothesis dissolves into a critical rant without any redeeming features. So, the following chapters offer some waypoints and suggestions before addressing the more difficult subject of 'People

Management' - with all that this subject implies.

None of it is a straight road; it will never be a straightforward journey; it is certainly not how you would expect a crow to fly. Life is not like that, the human condition is not like that and neither is the workplace. And with this in mind, there are a lot of issues to be examined, difficulties to encounter and problems to be raised with no guarantee of finding the truth. However, in work, as in life, we should never be afraid of running out of answers but running out of questions.

The Road Ahead

'Management Control' is an Oxymoron

'Management Control' is a phrase that is misused, misunderstood and has some woeful connotations. 'Control' is confused with power, authority, status and influence. It implies not only what is necessary for a Manager to achieve, it becomes a pre-requisite for Management success. Control is supposed to be about other people but it also about how much *power* a Manager can exert and the timescale in which decisions and direction are translated into physical actions or activities. The contradiction lies in the fact that 'Management' should be expressive, extrovert, creative and supportive; 'Control' on the other hand is restrictive, dogmatic, introverted and damaging.

Ask yourself: 'Am I in control?' Wouldn't we just love to say, 'yes'. Wouldn't we just love to have our fingers firmly held on a steadily ticking pulse – one that is generated by our own Managerial metronome? A constant tune where we decide the beat, the rhythm and everyone falls into place? If this was the case, wouldn't 'Management Control' actually become a self-fulfilling cycle of irritation and nonsense? We should ask whether Management Control is really an aspiration for which inordinate amounts of resource are used. Would we really like to build a corporate North Korea where adulation and subjugation is matched by ultimate power of thoughts, deeds and actions? Is that the path we want to tread? A situation where people value authority for fear of its consequence? Would we want people to respect authority for nothing else than for our own singular purpose?

Managers can perceive their role as trying to keep a lid on the evils of the world contained in Pandora's jar. It keeps many awake at night with the frightening possibilities. There is a constant fear of the evils of anarchy and the manifestation of 'chaos' is only a few steps away from a fully-fledged reality. And here lies another inconsistency - the true contradiction of the role of Management and organisational practice. By striving for control there is an urge to put a lock and key on an over-heightened version of mayhem. But from *chaos,* in its more liberal sense, comes innovation, creativity, individualism and new thinking. All the things that are seen as productive, inspiring and exciting. Chaos – turmoil, disorder or freedom - does not naturally precede anarchy.

Control is an imposition that breeds all sorts of organisational ailments and breeds a corporate culture of conservatism and pragmatism. "Don't rock the boat"; "Keep your head down"; "Don't say anything untoward" are as indicative of a need for subservience and control as anything else. The eagerness for control is indeed contradictory – there is frustration when people do not do as they are told and frustration when they are not forthcoming with suggestions; irritation when people make mistakes and annoyance when people are not innovative enough. By trying to impose control, we gain nothing; we fail in the long term; we block the tributaries of individual creativity and success whilst creating a dam of frustration and drowning a multitude of aspirations. Every attempt to impose 'control' has a subdued but powerfully negative effect.

One Company I know, after years of trying to impose some level of control, suddenly decided to 'engage' with people and mounted a suggestion box outside the canteen for Employees to contribute ideas on improving working conditions and efficiency. To the Management team's obvious annoyance, the box was almost always empty. The reaction to this was obvious and predictable: it was an affirmation that people needed to be told, needed to be directed and controlled because, in their own words: "They clearly can't think for themselves." A suggestion box can be a great incentive but when it is the only concession to Employee involvement it is treated with the same disdain as all other attempts to direct the way things are done.

"Everyone thinks of changing the world but no one thinks of changing himself" Leo Tolstoy

Vestiges or symptoms of autocracy and despotism, exist within any Company. We despair when actions are taken in the face of common sense with the apparently plausible excuse that they were 'told' to do it that way. There is a good reason why normally intelligent people decide to leave common sense at their door. It is usually because they have been conditioned to do so. When the parameters of control are established, there should be no surprise when people are afraid to supersede them.

The 'control' elements and parameters are not plastered on the wall; they are more discrete and obscure; they are not even mentioned or talked about. In corporations where everyone is struggling to climb the ladder of their own aspirations – or even hang on – just a fleeting word of dissent or equivocation can spell years in the wilderness; decisions become fudged with the rhetoric of political manoeuvring and actions draw the rebuke of those wiser and more astute. The arbitrary 'face that doesn't fit' becomes a metaphor for organisational re-shifting and the stamp of authority on individuals and the way they work.

Locked within this pursuit of control is the reliance on data and numbers. Control is confused with the dialogue of numbers. In fact, there is an absurd logic which leads many to believe that the surfeit of numbers – metrics and indices – is a proportional measure of control. The more numbers, the more data; the more data, the more information; the more information, the more control. Lots of numbers equals lots of control, which in turn equals good Management. The 'good' Managers are therefore the ones with numbers in their heads and at their fingertips. They are the ones who can produce answers to the most bizarre questions and produce the facts and figures to back them up.

The visible and tangible methods of control are engineered through Management Information Systems, assorted multi-coloured graphs, pie charts and trend analyses. The Management Control and Reporting System (MCRS) is often inflicted on organisations as a method by which Managers can 'control' their environments. The way it is sold can be misleading; the way it is used can be flawed; the way it is discarded because it doesn't provide the expected level of 'control' can be imprudent, especially when nothing else is in place. There is nothing wrong with numbers, systems and assorted indices – just the way they are employed. The MCRS should be a method of assessing the efficiency of the process within certain assumed parameters and allows Managers to deliberate and take actions to improve the stream of activities that are used to serve the end consumer – and no more. Data, information, systems and 'controls' are not there to as an *end* but a *means*. They do not bestow the right or presumption that people can be manipulated, restricted and 'controlled'. The language, for example, of 'labour controls' is used like a method of restraint and regulation. It is as though the 'dashboard', 'KPI's' 'trackers', 'evaluation methods' and other assorted paraphernalia of the knowledgeable Manager can be used to limit the natural curiosity and waywardness of the average human being. This is never going to be the case.

The need to be in 'control' is not just driven by the Manager but the outside world's perception of the role a Manager should undertake. When Managers have to admit they are not in control (either to themselves or to others) there is a reluctant admission that they are not the Managers they ought to be (or want to be) and that their lack of control is synonymous – or directly indicative – of their capacity and capability of being a Manager.

Fear is the parent of cruelty. Bertrand Russell

Control is elusive – and thankfully so. It is contradictory and a time-wasting pursuit taken by those with a misguided comprehension of the word and its implications. The bottom line is that Management control is not what we really want. We do not want automatons, we do not want subjugation, we do not like blind obedience and we recoil at the very idea of subservience. We dislike people always waiting for the 'green light' when the situation needs instant action and we want people to show some entrepreneurial spirit.

Many of the Managers I meet like to think they *are* in control and are willing to think and say as much. Whether it is down to optimism or low expectations it is clearly not the case. And that is the way it should be. Management control is not only an oxymoron, it is a blind alley – a dead end – for every Manager and their organisations.

"Firm but unfair"

Admittedly, it is not just the idea of 'control' but the pursuit of 'control' that is the problem. If actual control does not exist, then it is how Managers often try to enforce a version of this illusion. Whether it is achievable is purely academic to the person subjugated to the wiles and ambitions of those in search of absolute authority. If some Managers were honest, there would be an admission that imprinted on their imaginary job descriptions would be the words "discipline" and "retribution". There is always a place for a Manager to hold a firm hand, to make things explicit especially when there is a threat to production output, service levels and the values of the Company. However, there is an immediate problem when Managers unwittingly write "punishment" on their mental "to-do" lists and when the day doesn't seem as fulfilling unless an Employee has been the victim of some verbal abuse.

This can take on many guises: the quiet aside is taken as 'a warning'; the 'instruction', an order with dire consequences; a 'reminder of one's responsibility' is interpreted as a 'telling off', a 'gentle reminder' becomes a sharp rebuke and a 'little advice' can be putting someone in their place. Any explicit communication wears the double mask of perception and intention. But it is not just the circumstance in isolation but the climate it creates. Each occurrence is broadcast and amplified and though it might generally create the intended environment, it is ultimately destructive and overpowering. It can create a climate of fear - the pervasive trepidation becomes stifling and inhibits any genuine desire to take the initiative.

Power is often translated as the ability to bully, to intimidate, to frighten and to cajole. If this is in a Manager's dictionary it would not be acceptable. The pursuit of power, of control, of authority it not always in accordance with responsibilities and accountabilities and neither should it be. Influence sounds rational with the use of reasoned discussion rather than dogma or the blind rage of authority. Power used to subdue is nasty, and used in conjunction with control, generates all sorts of negative connotations.

Certainly, within any organisation trying to impose 'control' and 'authority', there is dishonesty, a distinct lack of information and engagement, selective and censured discussion, a reluctance to give feedback *upwards*, silos and cliques that are designed to consolidate and protect rather than involve and innovate.

The man who is denied the opportunity of taking decisions of importance begins to regard as important the decisions he is allowed to take. C.Northcote Parkinson

Power, authority, dominance, 'control' and executive muscle is sought by people who don't have it - and feel it is an essential part of the fabric of Management. Power and authority is pursued by those who believe it to be a fortress where they can be left unchallenged, where they can be impervious to threats of dissention and others' creativity; and ultimately that power by itself provides confidence. Conversely, it is easy to believe that the absence of power engenders low-esteem.

Power can be wielded as a threat, to impose fear and trepidation as though the worst punishment imaginable is imminent. In a state of totalitarianism, the onslaught of propaganda and the single-minded drive to capture a population's sanity will always be a lid on a seething, boiling pot of indignation. In religious communities and establishments, the fear of unorthodoxy and agnosticism is countered by the ominous dread of supernatural and eternal consequences. It is not surprising that megalomaniacs are seen as a deities first and a leader second – it makes everyone's work so much easier. If you cannot conquer people's spirit by earthly means... Fortunately, Managers do not have spiritual damnation as a useful threat and cannot call upon divine intervention or punishment in the afterlife - but I have met a few who would grab the opportunity with both hands.

The whole point of fear and punishment is to introduce a mandate for power and control. What we really should be looking for is *influence*. Real power is achievement through invited influence; real power is creativity; rewarded power is respect. Power comes through delegation; power comes through involvement, through acknowledgement, shared risk-taking and respect for others. Engagement is power by softer means. But how different 'power' sounds compared to 'empower': two opposite ends of the same scale. With the perception of control and the assumption of power, there is an urge to keep information, to do things rather than delegate, to instigate a regime of retribution and to stifle initiative – in fact all the things that make people less productive, less inspired, less loyal - and *less* empowered.

When organisations seek to empower and engage Employees, it is the intention and perception that can be quite different – as well as the underlying ethos. For example: *power* and authority is something to which *I, as a Manager, am entitled*; Employee *empowerment* is something that *they must earn and which can be given and taken away*. Empowerment should be about shared responsibility and shared development in services and products. In reality, and based on the wrong beliefs, it can easily end up as little more than an extra missive on the notice board. There has to be a method and approach by which confrontation is turned into cooperation and the goals of all the individuals are understood and shared - when power becomes an unwanted diversion and authority an unnecessary distraction.

Who is my customer?

Why is there such an urge to impose authority when the job is to create the conditions for people to succeed? Surely it is in the best interests of everyone to adopt a different approach? The urge to play 'master and servant' shares its own set of risks but would never be suggested as a winning formula to ensuring the best conditions for Employees. A complete shift would be to imagine Managers asking all Employees a very simple question: 'What do you need from me (us) to make the day successful?' It is not just that this could be a good idea – it is the resulting behaviours and consequence of not doing it! It is not an approach that could be taken 'given the right conditions' but an opportunity immediately lost when *not* grasped with both hands. Time, resource, resolve and effort is wasted when Managers and Employees move in different orbits.

"Those who cannot change their minds cannot change anything". George Bernard Shaw

So, who is the customer? Who should I, as a Manager prioritise? I was once in a Company that had failed on a new product launch. The product did not meet the specification and the agreed volumes had not been shipped. The *Customer*, quite rightly, was incensed. Of course, general panic ensued which meant that the operational Management team left their desks and offices and scurried down to the shop floor to find the cause of the problem and how it could have been averted. It was an unexpected set of circumstances and a repetition of the same events was unthinkable. After a number of conference calls and meetings, a plan of action was drafted whilst the Customer was assured that the catalogue of errors would not be repeated. The issues were 'resolved' and the general fever of panic abated as everything returned to normal. The next day, the same mistakes happened again.

The problem was that the people on the lines – those actually making the product - has not been involved. Not at all! The message given was: 'This is a new product, get on with it!' They had not been consulted on the launch, they had not been informed of the sensitivity of the new product, they had not been issued with the correct specification on the line (which, of course meant that they had no idea when they were doing things incorrectly) they were not even made aware there was a problem, that the order had been fouled up, that the Customer was up in arms and that they had to do something quite different. They didn't even know who the Customer was! They only knew something was terribly wrong. Why else would a group of panicked Managers descend to the production floor? The product launch, the sensitivity, the issues, the complaints, solutions, actions and customer promises were not communicated to the very people who were supposed to implement them. Which is why the same mistakes were repeated the very next day. It seems absurd to focus primarily on the end Customer and not on the people who are providing the means by which that service can be delivered.

If the people carrying out the work are considered to be the primary Customer, the 'end Customer' (the people paying for the product) has a better chance of receiving what was ordered. If the Employee is ignored, the end result is always left to chance. By serving the real customer - the Employees - the Manager's role achieves a new simplicity rather than the one that is continually being compromised and marginalised. The myriad of tasks deemed as imperatives become superfluous and unnecessary. By advocating the default description of Management as *creating the conditions for people to succeed*, the task falls into the understandable parameters of providing the tools, equipment, training and environment for Employees to achieve 'what needs to be achieved'. By considering Employees as customers, the language changes. Instead of: "What have you done?" the authoritarian, controlling approach is transformed to become: "What can I do to help?"

From an environment and organisation that favours an autocratic method of getting the best out of people, this may take an enormous dose of humility. However, by making Employees greater, bigger and better, the organisation becomes so much stronger. And the stronger you make your customer (the Employee), the stronger you become yourself. The converse is as true and instantly more recognisable. By gauging the levels of success against a brow-beaten army of forsaken Employees, Managers have to use all their powers of resilience and limits of their patience to keep the ship afloat. Not only are all parties exhausted or disinterested, the ship becomes rudderless and wayward. "Our people are our greatest asset" should not be a clichéd strapline but a statement of intent. Authority comes with the trust of Employees; power (shared power) comes from the combined weight of consensus and shared objectives. And, if this intention is to be carried out in practice, it requires examination of how Managers communicate, discuss and share ideas and how Managers spend their time. It involves commitment, and support; it involves a change in the environment and the parameters by which the external, secondary customer can be served. It requires a change of mind; a change in perceptions and the way Managers like to behave. It is a pathway that has its traps and diversions like any other but it has tangible benefits that have an enormous effect on the efficiency and success of the organisation and the business. Consider people first: their needs, their requirements, their lives and livelihoods which are the heart and soul of every good organisation.

Do you like People?

The question, 'do you like people?' seems banal and slightly incongruous. Nonetheless, it is quite an important one. The answer not only indicates the predilection to physical and intellectual interaction with people but also indicates a predisposition to ensuring whether Employees can and will prosper. So many organisations have become distant and unfamiliar with the people in their care, the people who keep the lines running, those who answer the phones and those maintaining the machines. 'Liking' people is represented, not as a pre-requisite but a potential hindrance to success; a possible stumbling block in the race for promotion and success. People are regarded as a resource in the same way as raw materials, electricity and machinery; a means by which products can be assembled, packaged and shipped. People have become a diversion, an unnecessary and awkward waste of a Manager's time. In response, disproportionately sized HR departments have grown to fill the gap to be surrogate Managers - to ease the flow of communication and to do the things that Managers generally do not want to do or believe they do not have the time to do. This includes training, interviews, briefings, grading structures, skill reviews, disciplinary meetings and counselling.

Was there a time that familiarity with people bred a reciprocal dependency? Was there a time when the word 'loyalty' went hand in hand with the sense of community? Not, not really. It was all a myth. And yet loyalty has become a bone of contention as Employees re-evaluate the importance of the Company for which they work and instead prioritise their own well-being. Job security is a thing of the past and the notion of a 'career for life' is seen as a veiled threat rather than an absolute ambition.

Perhaps it is a symptom of our Neanderthal past that makes us behave and sound like cavemen first thing in the morning. There is a touching reluctance and apathy that colours the faces of those that endure the hard trek into the office, the factory, the call centre and the retail park. Standing next to the main road that conveys people into the city centre every morning, it is difficult to find someone smiling; it is harder to catch a person with a sparkle in their eye and almost impossible to see a look of expectant anticipation. Behind every Employee perhaps, there is a fun-loving human-being struggling to get out... It is said that the incidence of heart attacks rises sharply on a Monday morning. Maybe it is the stress, the pressure, the monotony or nature's calling card to say that this is not what life should be about. Besides, why on earth would you have a coronary at the weekend?

I would wager that given the choice, most commuters would rather have stayed at home when in fact there should be a hundred good reasons why people turn up for work every day; there should be at least fifty reasons why people should not feel the urge to run for the door at the end of normal working hours; there should, at least, be a few positive things to tell their family at home. Is this because people do not feel valued, do not feel appreciated or even liked?

The 'asset' that many Senior Executives feel compelled to mention in the last slide of the deck, is to remind everyone that their latest accomplishment, painted in excruciating detail, could not have been achieved without their people. It still sounds as laboured and disingenuous the last time I heard it as much as the first. Why is it not the first slide and why does it always sound like an afterthought brought on by convention rather than conviction? An asset is something you take care of, something you hold as precious and which contains an intrinsic value. An asset carries obligations and accountabilities.

The Moral Dimension?

There is a simple but disregarded axiom of everyday employment: Employees are a number of hours older at the end of their shift than when they started. It seems too obvious to warrant a mention. And yet, within the simplicity of that statement lies a serious and important truth: people spend a good deal of their waking lives trying to earn a living, enough to eat, a roof over their head and enough to keep themselves warm. They are hours of their lives - hours of a day that can never be re-captured. As such, they are valuable and precious and more valuable and precious than we like to acknowledge. For with that acknowledgement comes the responsibility by which a Manager is obligated underlining the primary definition of the Manager's role. The recognition of this premise shifts the emphasis of duty from someone *presiding* over a person's efforts to *enabling* people experience a level of achievement. It is the ability to ensure that Employees understand that the hours spent at work have been worthwhile and appreciated.

As it stands, we invite armies of worker into factories to

do a job of work in places where it can be cold and damp, hot and sweaty, claustrophobic, dark and with no natural light. They are offered the lowest wage, with no proper instruction or the best equipment, no proper facilities, canteens, lockers or clothing and then are expected to meet Company requirements, standards, rules and regulations, organisational targets and output rates. The reality is that this is *their* day, this is *their* job and this is *their* life. Many work in soul-destroying conditions and through fortune, circumstance or hard work, Managers have the authority and opportunity to make it so much worse. To spend hours in an uncomfortable environment is one thing – to feel that it has not been acknowledged or appreciated seems so much more wasteful and destructive. Alan W. Kennedy wrote: "If every day at work feels like a Friday, then you are doing what you were meant to do." Yes, but when everyone in the Company *longs* for every day to be Friday, that is quite different.

I have worked in places that could be used as background images for Dante's Inferno and archaic offices that have been recreated from a Dickens novel; places of work that are as cold as a fridge and as wet as holiday in Manchester. I have worked in offices that are sub-tropical on the sunniest days when the air-conditioner refuses to work and in factories where the canteen is the dimmest afterthought of an oblivious architect. They betray the priorities of those in charge and cast a sharp shadow on the interests that

Management have towards the welfare and safety of the people in their care. I must also add that I have worked in places that have been taken from a furniture catalogue and where the floors are so clean, you could eat your dinner from them; where the seating would put any good hotel to shame and where the food on offer compares with some very good restaurants. The simple conclusion is that it is not just the backdrop that shapes the organisation but the way people are treated within them. The sense of frustration, lack of involvement, the silence of non-existent communication can be just as intense in a fully-fitted office from Ikea than a gritty steelworks. By not making people part of the workplace, by not including them in any conversation, taking an interest, giving them a sense of achievement, do we make their day better or worse? Do we add or subtract?

The lack of interest is as dispiriting whatever the size and condition of the building. The snippets of dialogue are judged by their sincerity regardless of the furnishings. When "Thanks for today" are the first words spoken at the *end* of the day, it is generally considered to be a platitude and usually taken as such. Concessions to interaction can be a mere nod of the head or the ubiquitous series of posters resplendent with stunning wildlife photography, complete with insincere quotes about 'teambuilding', 'motivation' and 'inspiration', hung in various strategic places, either to brighten up the area, hide the damp spot or as a gesture of corporate intent.

**People are infected by many mad principles... infecting them with niceness should be child's play.
Richard Dawkins**

This self-inflicted distance, this archaic divide perpetuates the attitude that Employees are the fodder by which the Company can succeed. It is this detachment that pervades and distorts the culture of the Company, making it difficult to listen to the expectations of those doing the work and those who are supposed to be managing. As humans we have always cooperated – it is the making of us as a species. We would not have been able to survive otherwise. So while it is often claimed to be an overriding purpose, why is it that organisations try to foster something else?

The appreciation we have of people and the imperative of appreciating people's energy and vitality should not stem from pragmatism alone. The engagement of people and interest in their welfare should not be prioritised just because it can give the business the best results – there are much more important and pressing motives and much nobler intentions. People have more importance than tools, equipment, processes and systems. It is an impossible task to empower people, raise their expectations, inspire and attempt to value their efforts whilst at the same time devalue their exertions with banalities; by paying lip service to working as a team; through attempting to 'control' them, through re-engineering or by 'lean' strategies. This does nothing more than undermine those to whom empowerment and engagement should be directed.

An unhealthy climate can easily be induced by the notion of status and power. Work (manual or unskilled for example) can so easily be viewed as laborious, tedious and undemanding and therefore words like achievement and accomplishment seem at odds with what people actually do. The way people are recognised and rewarded dictates the way people behave. When there is a greater focus on costs and productivity alone, there should be no surprise that the investment in people is low and that morale is even lower. Morals and morale become intertwined and self-generating.

"Those Agency people – they're just temporary aren't they?"

I was conducting an appraisal in a food preparation area – a study in their processes, systems and behaviours. It was nothing out of the ordinary – a simple analysis as a precursor to a full scale project. I noticed that some people on the lines tended to drift away after an initial flurry of activity. I asked the supervisor what was happening, "Oh, they have nothing to do with me", she replied, "They're *Agency*".

Agency workers are commonplace. In some organisations they are the cornerstone in a measured strategy to curb labour costs, to increase flexibility and to keep the factory running in times of pre-supposed volatility. Agency staff are seen as a necessary evil and the source of a myriad of excuses for why the factory is not running at its optimum. The names and faces are ticks in the box and allocated like random numbers in a lottery. There seems to be an unwritten but widely acknowledged mantra: "I Manage my people, I 'make do' with Temps."

This is not just a moral and social issue - it contains its own economic imperatives, especially when Agency staff can account for more than 50% of labour costs. Agency workers are seen as professional vagrants – cheap and convenient. However, even though the costs may seem low in comparison, the numbers in total are a considerable expense to any Company. This begs the question: why would any business allocate such a high percentage of costs for resources to which there is attached such little importance, so little attention and so little expectation? With little in the form of induction, training or familiarisation, Agency workers are sent on the production lines amidst the noise and bustle of the floor, often in an uninviting, unforgiving environment with the assumption that they can 'just get on with it.'

Most organisations have an induction programme in place, though granted, this is usually conducted by the Agency bureau themselves, whose principal commitment and business model is to service the customers with the correct numbers – and not necessarily those who are best suited. Introduction to the production lines can be woeful and demonstrates the worst aspects of current

Management practice. I have seen people in food preparation areas who, quite literally, have been given a knife and told to cut whatever came down the line. Maybe as a result of time, language or pressing priorities, matters such as productivity, yield, wastage, contamination and health and safety are left to one side. To some extent, this is understandable – "Besides", I have heard Supervisors say, "They may not turn up again"; "They might just be there for the day"; "Maybe they will find an alternative place to work?" *And who would blame any of them?*

Equally, I have known of Agency workers driving many miles each day in all sorts of weather with no guarantee of work or even the minimum number of hours. I have known Agency people religiously turning up in a way that puts their permanent counterparts to shame. I have seen Agency workers stay behind to make sure the work is completed for the day, unbound by normal working hours and the rush for the gate at the end of the shift and who keep to the rules and regulations that are often ignored by more experienced staff. All this, I have to say, in spite of any Management attention. There is an obvious but not inexplicable paradox here. There are some who are clearly able to demonstrate degrees of workmanship regardless of what levels of expectation are given them. It is based on hard-headedness, familiarity and some degree of trust. Many are desperate to get their next pay packet. Surely such determination is commendable? The expectation is not of any recognition or reward other than being asked to come again and earn what they can. The pragmatism and necessity of their predicament overcomes any sensitivity regarding contribution and involvement.

The fact is that Agency workers are the first point of call in the event of any cost-cutting exercise. It is not only a natural course of action but also a legal requirement. The irony is that many of the Agency workers, whose services might no longer be required, may well offer a rich bounty in terms of their commitment, skills, intelligence and education - if only they were given the chance! If only they had an opportunity to demonstrate their potential. This is not just to engender a feeling of well-being or belonging. By making Permanent and Agency staff an integral part of the workplace and creating the right conditions to succeed, there is a natural and proven correlation to productivity, quality, health and safety, team spirit and achievement. It is the foundation on which expectations, targets and delivery of a good day's work should be made. It is nigh on impossible to fully implement values of quality, productivity and safety when there is one rule for the permanent staff and quite another for Agency; when people turn a blind eye to the shortcomings of Agency workers (due to the lack of engagement) and expect everyone else to compensate. There is little expectation of Agency Workers which is a natural reflection of the reluctance to treat them as bona-fide members of a team and integral to the success of the business. In its purest sense, the best Managers are not those who simply work with the most skilled and productive but those who can inspire the weakest; not those who only spend time with the people they know but those who spend the time getting to know the people they don't. It is a simple matter of good manners and common decency – a consequence of liking people. Equally, it is a matter of economics and productivity as well as good and sound Management practice.

"They're only here for the money!"

Money is the only reward because that is the only thing on offer. If the aim is to feed the pocket – not the mind, the body or the soul - should we wonder why people are starved of humour, cooperation, engagement and creativity? Money as a prime motivator is widely accepted and, in terms of Management behaviour, widely adopted and welcomed. It is easy enough to clutch at evidence to back up the claim and once embraced as a conviction, leads to a myriad of techniques and behaviours that are counterproductive and illogical, however consistent and superficially plausible. It becomes entrenched – and if not a truth – becomes an embedded belief that becomes unshakable.

The attitude deeply ingrained throughout many organisations is geared towards payment and the wage bill as though it is the only enticement that holds any interest for an Employee. This avenue leads Managers away from the essential principle that people can achieve beyond normal expectations and possess a vast array of talents and skills.

When money is the principal motivator, it is due to the conditions created by Company policy and a reflection of an archaic attitude towards Employees. The proposition that money is the only interest of Employees betrays more about the person who holds it to be true. A Manager once said to me in passing: 'They only make an issue of things when money is involved', which, I thought, exposed more about the position in which an Employee was placed, emphasising the distance between employer and Employee, rather than any desperate demand for more pay. 'They only seem to be creative when they feel there is more money in it' begs the question about the circumstances that have been created. The resulting circle of frustration, exasperation and self-fulfilling beliefs become more evident. At best, people perform to their ability before they find something else. At worst, staff under-perform in a climate of low expectations.

Money, it turned out, was exactly like sex, you thought of nothing else if you didn't have it and thought of other things if you did. James Baldwin

Again, we could ask the question: *who could blame any of them?* When everyone has only the next pay-packet to look forward to against a backdrop of incessant marketing, advertising and aspirational acquisitions. The creed of consumerism has taken hold where the belief in essentials and 'food on the table', left off. Greed was never 'good', it just became acceptable and 'keeping up' was substituted by 'being one step ahead'. This search for new challenges, excitement and novelty eagerly spills over into people's career paths and chosen professions. There is always a desire to find something else, something more stimulating, more inspirational and rewarding – why not a new car, a new house, a new boss, a new job? But it is worth considering why some in higher positions in the organisation believe that others – Employees and colleagues alike - have such different motives than their own?

Herzberg argued that there are 'Hygiene' needs (or maintenance factors) and 'Motivators'. Company policy, contact with their Supervisors, work conditions (there is only so much a person can tolerate), status, security, relationship with subordinates, personal life and salary were 'maintenance' factors but these were not 'motivators' - they did not impel people to act over and above requirements. Herzberg believed the true motivators were quite separate and included: achievement, recognition, the work itself, responsibility and advancement. In his studies, Herzberg believed that the wage packet has its own share of complexity but concluded that money is not a *motivator* in the same way as the primary motivators such as achievement and recognition. In fact, they can be significant *de-*

motivators. *"Viewed within the context of the sequences of events, salary as a factor belongs more in the group that defines the job situation and is primarily a dissatisfier."*

By saying 'do that' and I will give you 'this' sustains the simplest pretext and misguided myth: that most people are unwilling to do something without reward. It presumes that Employees are mercenaries and the person in charge is the 'fixer'. By having a bag of 'goodies', 'rewards' and 'appetisers', the Manager is allowed to get away with the real job of understanding the person and creating the right environment for them to willingly succeed. It also forms a convenient battlefield where Employee representatives (unions and shop stewards) and employers create the boundaries and justify their relative positions. 'Skill Reviews' and 'Organisational Changes' become arguments about pay and demarcation. It becomes a tangible agenda rather than encouraging the more diffuse ideas of *happiness, achievement, contribution* and *fulfilment*.

The conviction that 'They're only here for the money' is supported by the fact that people are more than willing to resign if more money is on offer elsewhere. But surely, if a Manager, a Department or Organisation can create the conditions for *money* to be the sole motivator, it can also create the conditions by which other factors can determine an Employee's engagement? It becomes a convoluted trap: Employees are kept happy by paying them enough and, if possible, more than the competition. It becomes a 'selling point' to maintain the staff the organisation would like to keep. As a result, payment becomes the central issue and discussion point which in turn becomes transformed into tangible evidence that money is all people are interested in. This idea conveys a set of rules that shapes a Manager's attitude to the whole gamut of traditional tasks such as discipline, rewards, guidance, education and development. Money, with the pay packet as a principal driver, is a good excuse not to Manage.

The Tyranny of Bonuses

The belief that payment is a prime motivator becomes even more contentious when it is Company policy to reward staff with bonuses. Is it not the case that bonus payments are in fact, Management by proxy? The decision lies between whether people should be managed properly and whether they should be paid a bonus. The administrative gymnastics that decide *which* people qualify or *how* they qualify, on the scale of extra payments, is as soulless as it is a dereliction of Management responsibility and endeavour. Why do so many people pin their hopes on bonuses and why do Managers see this as their only contribution to the loyalty and productivity of staff? Why are bonuses paid? Is it for the benefit of Managers or for their Employees? Is it because the normal reward is unsatisfactory? Is it a carrot that diverts people's attention away from their slavish conditions? Or is it an appetiser that diverts

Employees' attention from the competition? Is it right that bonuses become so embedded that they become part of the mainstream culture, act as a Managerial surrogate and become tools of Managerial 'control'? There is an accepted condescension in the way that the 'barrel of seed', is thrown out as befitting people's perceived performance, ranking and attitude.

Naturally, there will always be those who have made real efforts but find there is no more in the 'pot'. The method and system of the scheme and the massive expectations that come with it, casts a shadow over the organisation and can easily cause all goodwill and energy to evaporate. It becomes destructive and demoralising. The weight of *one* person's disappointment can influence the mood, the aspirations and moment of joy for the *many*; the elation of *one* can cause resentment within the crowd. The knife edge of reward becomes all too evident and is exposed as the Management weapon of choice. Bonuses, by their very nature, are manipulative and as they become binding, they become indispensable. The fact is, people don't necessarily need bonuses - they *do* need recognition.

If that is not enough, enormous amounts of time, effort and bureaucracy are expended to keep the wheels in motion. The remaining machinery of Management comes to a shuddering halt as all attention is focused on this one motivational gimmick. The Manager has to pose as either a bureaucratic Father Christmas or the Ghost of Christmas past. Once the bonus and the pay packet becomes the default Management trick, it leads to a sorry world of alienation and misaligned aspirations.

So, what is the alternative? How do you make a system less divisive? Does it not depend on the culture you want to make? The simple principle of *achievement* is at the heart of all good organisations. What is left is a justifiable argument that says that people need to be motivated or *inspired* 'by other means'.

"There are a lot of people I just can't be bothered motivating".

People's inability to succeed is often compounded by their Manager spreading the word of their failure. It is easier for people to proclaim that people are 'useless' rather than saying, 'they have made some mistakes but I am going to work with them to make them so much better.' The incompetence of others is a much more convenient way to explain poor results and draws attention to the struggles with which any Manager has to cope. It works by gaining sympathy and deflecting attention from the more important imperative of doing something about the situation.

I am not one to believe that everyone *can* or *will* succeed but I believe everyone should have a chance given the right circumstances. That is not to say that a person should be allowed to make as many mistakes as they wish but is it really *fair* to question a person's ability to succeed in conditions that are not conducive or ineffectual? Is it not best to improve any situation, give

Employees the necessary environment, encouragement time and resource before making judgements on their potential? Let's face it, the people who *appear* to be succeeding are those who have just learnt to cope in difficult conditions.

The trouble is, there are many who feel that by 'pushing' they are also *managing* regardless of the circumstances and environment. By giving impetus against an otherwise static object, there is an infused satisfaction that something worthwhile is being done that is of value. The concept of motivation is synonymous with 'driving' and 'cajoling', 'persuasion' and 'exhortation' when there should be something quite different. I was recently reminded of one of Aesop's Fables about the North Wind and the Sun. As with all good bed time stories, they are relevant to children and adults in equal measure - or in other words, they are children's stories with a morality that adults are skilfully adept at ignoring.

On observing a man walking down the street, the sun and the wind, disputing which was stronger, decided on a wager: they would compete to be the first to take the coat off the man and the one who succeeded would be considered stronger than the other. The North Wind gathered all its strength and blew as hard as he could causing the man to wrap his coat around him, shielding himself against the fearsome blasts. The more he blew, the more tightly the man fastened his coat. The North Wind, exhausted, decided to give the sun a chance. The sun shone brightly in the sky at which the man began to perspire and quickly took off the coat to cool himself down.

It is an unsophisticated tale pitching coercion against empathy but not forgetting that people naturally and unconsciously react to environmental conditions. The essence of this story is not what people want *others* to do but how people will react to outside influence. Managers believe they have to 'do' something to their subordinates to get them to 'do' things. The hindrance or leap of faith is the unwillingness to accept that people are prepared to do more than they are paid for; that they have more to offer; that they want to achieve more; that they have an inner core of talent and a deep pool of potential.

Hawthorn demonstrated the power of observation and the simple act of taking an interest but this was only a temporary phenomenon lasting as long as the person is watched. The knowledge that someone is genuinely interested in what is being done, how it is being done and the results that are achieved is more sustainable and more substantial than a direct command or 'push' in the right direction.

The expectation brings about the expected. John Maynard Keynes

What is needed is the energy and enthusiasm to 'ignite' and to inspire. To *inspire* is to create an environment where a person wants to pursue their own success, their own interpretation of achievement and not necessarily the goals and targets created by others.

All this can sound extremely credulous and simplistic. There is an implication of conviction and there is a prerequisite of faith - not necessarily a faith that all people can achieve their potential but that most people can and will succeed. Most people, given the right conditions, will surprise the best of us. To use the pretext that only a *few* will succeed should not be used as an excuse for not investing in anyone at all; to use the failure of a few to justify the lack of effort for the many is a poor defence against the imperatives and responsibilities of being a great Manager.

Creating a true framework takes effort, dedication, foresight, discipline and a certain amount of stubbornness. There is little room for scepticism in creating the conditions for others to succeed. Employees are a mixed bunch: some people are born awkward, others have awkwardness thrust upon them; others are troublesome, antagonistic and just 'hard work'. And yet, in general, people generally do not need to be forced into a state of happiness, of goodness, of being pleasant and of being accommodating – but it takes so little effort to steer them away and cause them to be obstreperous. People react to expectation – good or bad, fair or unfair, implicit or inferred.

Only by knowing the person is it easier to understand their potential and what makes them 'tick'. To *inspire* involves understanding the person, their interests, their ambitions and their limitations – and not just in the workplace. It takes time and willingness – and sometimes with people you don't necessarily like. Which brings us back to the earlier point: I don't believe you have to necessarily like each person but you *must* like people.

"What I really want to do when I grow up..."

There are armies of hard-working people within organisations who, given half the chance, would rather be doing something else. They possess the skills, the talent and more essentially, the passion for pastimes other than the duties they are asked to perform for eight, solid hours every day. To the majority, the thought of losing their one source of income and sense of 'belonging' overrides their inner desire to explore new possibilities and pursue something more rewarding and in keeping with their talents. Too often it is security; too often it is the foggy uncertainty of the future; too often it is the means; too often it is a misplaced sense of loyalty. None of this, of course, can be dismissed; none of this is trivial.

None climbs so high as he who knows not whither he is going. Oliver Cromwell

The problem is that this army of people exists without anyone fully recognising who they are. To those Leaders who believe they have the unreserved attention of a host of grateful Employees charged with filling their personal pockets, think again; to those who believe that all Employees place the Company's interests before their own, there has to be an admission that this might be wide of the mark. Completing the necessary probation period does not mean that people give up their pipe dreams, their hopes, their ambitions and consign their imaginations to lock and key. For those who feel they should be 'doing something else', there will always be a boiling mixture of dissatisfaction, exasperation and at times resentment that life has not given them the opportunity, the wherewithal or freedom of purpose to seek the life they really wanted. Every now and again, there is a story of someone who hands in their resignation to go off and try their hand at painting, to travel, or do some voluntary work. Often, it is completely unexpected to those who are in charge. 'Who'd have thought it?' people say. Well, as it turns out, quite a few should have *known* about it. Many think the person has gone a bit mad because they cannot equate the quiet administrator with anyone creative, spontaneous or *brave*. To others, there is that deep-seated envy of not trying it themselves. To any Manager, it should not have been a surprise if they had an inkling of the 'real' person they had in their charge.

It would be wrong to suggest that Managers should be career advisors but at least they should have an understanding of what it is that people really want from their life: security, peace of mind, a challenge, promotion, recognition, a technical or managerial role, more responsibility or another job? It is a vital part of understanding why people react as they do, why they behave in their own special way. Equally, how they can make a greater contribution. Not all are necessarily able to achieve those ambitions but to treat them as unimaginative subordinates is to do them the greatest disservice and covers no one in glory.

On occasion, people are kept tethered to their work as though forgotten. There is little incentive to address those who have been placed in a strange, suspended state of animation - those who feel locked or 'trapped' in a circle of non-achievement, stress and low self-esteem. This is not only detrimental to the individual concerned but also for their colleagues and the Company as a whole. It is certainly no secret to the person in question or their colleagues, however much a Manager wishes to turn a blind eye. Besides, there must be a good reason why they have kept on for so long? There must be something they are doing that is important? They are permanent fixtures, left to their own devices who seem to avoid most of the downsizing regimes and instead of being moved out, are moved to one side. The cloak of 'efficiency drives' or executive 'cost cutting' measures should not be abused but neither should the search for humanity be usurped by misplaced charity. Some may call the workplace a 'sanctuary' but a business should not become a refuge for the misplaced, forgotten, the unhappy nor the incompetent.

Once the decision of redundancy is made, I have witnessed those with a palpable sense of relief on their faces but it would be wrong to suggest there are always good outcomes. There are not always 'happy endings' and for many the consequence is not that fortunate. Yet, there is no excuse to consign people to a lifetime in a job they despise, in which they cannot thrive and which destroys their soul.

It takes courage to take a personal interest in each Employee, it also takes more than compassion to ask people to explore different career paths, however ironic or euphemistic that might sound. Otherwise a Company can be left with Employees who have nowhere left to go, like wayward travellers, who have never been given a map and a compass, who remain where they are, hoping that someone will provide a new direction.

Interviews are just the start

The main reason we allow ourselves to ask such searching questions in an interview is because there is an increased sense of objectivity and interest. Who is this person? What are their strengths and weaknesses? *Who* would they work well with? Who would they *not* work well with? What are their hobbies and how do they spend their free time? What excites them? What annoys them? There are a multitude of questions based on professional diligence and natural curiosity. We are comfortable enough to go the extra step and examine the hopes and dreams of the person we have in front of us. We are flattered by the interest and respect they show us. After all, we are the 'gate keepers', the one physical barrier between them and a job they presumably, really want. Most of all, of course, we allow ourselves to become the interested and curious person we should be on a consistent basis.

Despite the congratulations when a suitable candidate has been hired, there is a lingering tinge of uncertainty. Are we totally convinced that the searching questions elicited the correct response? Are they as they appeared? Was it an open and honest account - or a charade? Of course, we wait and see; the bright-eyed aspirant is let loose into a world of conflicting messages, differing perceptions, divergent objectives and the sway of success and failure. Once they are employed what do they dream of next?

We must view young people not as empty bottles to be filled, but as candles to be lit. Robert H. Shaffer

The administrative details are obligingly dealt with, there is a tour, an introduction to other departments, perhaps a quick induction session until, eventually, the new Employee enters the door leading to their daily routine.

In some companies, there are evaluations; in some, there are follow-up meetings when new recruits are asked how they are getting on after which, the level of curiosity and interest dwindles... The period of 'fitting in' and initiation commences when the new starter is allowed to become immersed in the *accepted* but *unofficial* values and practices in the organisation and are allowed to adopt all the characteristics against which Management have been valiantly fighting. When things don't work out and the budding new intake seems to become anonymous and ordinary, there is an inclination to compare the hopeful *interviewee* with the current *employee* and wonder where things went wrong. It is not uncommon to hear:

"I think it was a mistake hiring them."

"Seems to have turned out just like the rest."

"They were really good at the interview, but if you ask me..."

"Well, he (or she) hasn't proved to be anything special."

"I caught so and so clocking off early the other day, with all the others."

"You leave them alone to get on with it and see what happens!"

It becomes more expedient and more comfortable to believe that the interview was a façade and that that the candidate was 'all style with little substance'. In retrospect, the promise of a new challenge, 'one hundred percent' support, regular training, back-up and scope for new responsibilities appear to be the promises lacking substance whilst the critical parts of the interview become clouded and forgotten:

"If we were to offer you a position, what would you expect of us?"

"Support?"

"Absolutely, one of our core values".

"Opportunities?"

"Certainly. That's how I got here!"

"Respect?"

"Without question, we value all our Employees."

"Encouragement to be involved in how the Company works?"

"One of our main principles".

"Training?"

"Something we pride ourselves on".

On reflection, the common failures made by the new recruit, could pale into insignificance. There is almost a perverse Darwinian mentality that picks the right Employee and then lets them just 'get on with it' to see whether they rise above the crowd, to see whether they sink or swim or whether they buckle under the pressure. "We've picked you out of the crowd, but let's see whether you survive in our organisation!" The new candidate can be swamped very quickly.

Taking on a new person is one way of accelerating the hopes and ambitions of an organisation – to create the best conditions rather than have the new aspirant drown in them. It is the greatest opportunity to *shape* the organisation not just by adopting accepted practice but by making use of a new pair of eyes and a newfound enthusiasm to do the job in the best way possible. Recruitment, guidance and support is the chance to change an essential ingredient of the culture which shapes, directs and drives the organisation.

Shaping the Environment

"Time Management is not something I've got round to."

Our careers are measured in time. Days are duly apportioned; revolving, cyclical periods that create their own gravities; bite-sized chunks of the day that demand carefully calibrated snippets of concentration. It is not necessarily the importance of events but their familiarity; not necessarily the human content but the habitual routines that receive the most attention.

The greatest challenge for any organisation is to make it possible for Managers and Supervisors to carry out the very duties for which they were hired. The care and attention of people is pushed to one side and only done when there is a gap in the hectic schedule or 'later in the day'. It is a task only considered when everything else is done: the reading of emails; talking to the boss and colleagues, looking at reports and analysing data, attending meetings and answering the phone. If Management is dealing with people in a meaningful and constructive way then it is still illuminating to observe what people want to manage instead: the budget, the accounts, the Kpi's, the overtime reports, machinery and kit, their desks, their schedules, finding out about their own peers – and yes, their own boss. There are a myriad of excuses made to avoid the essential core of the job. *It is a strange truism that Managers treat as less essential, the very things that are the most vital.*

Speaking to people, asking how they are doing, asking about their family, asking about their health, the job in hand, what needs to be done that day, future projects, future opportunities...the trouble is – it all takes time! If only the words: 'What my people really need from me today is...' was on the lips of every Manager first thing in the day.

There is an unremitting predicament: is it more important to spend time around what needs to done or organised around the expectation of others? Is the day organised around what is important and urgent or what other people insist is pressing and vital? Is it about perceived requirements or what is actually required as a Manager? Using the definition of the role of a Manager – 'creating the right conditions for people to thrive' - how much of the day is spent actually *creating* those right conditions?

Instead, a Manager may well be more inclined to say: "I have a number of meetings I need to attend"; "There are emails I have to respond to"; "There are reports I have to write" and, if there is any time after that... 'Well maybe I can go down to the shopfloor, into the General Office, into the workplace'? How much time spent in meetings would be superfluous if more was spent with people who actually knew what was going on?

Consciously or unconsciously, the imperatives of people's needs become less pressing and urgent than the attendance at meetings, the requirements of administration, the demands of suppliers, the necessities of Projects – and of course, the kaleidoscopic demands of the organisation. The tidy desk, the uniform regiment of files, the empty in-trays, the meticulously placed phones, calendars, stamps, pens and assorted Managerial trinkets, all neatly aligned, ready for the next impending executive decision. It is the routine, the self-imposed discipline that leads to a feeling of satisfaction – and there is nothing wrong with that - except when it directly intervenes with what is important and what is imperative. No one is perfect but there are some who believe that orderliness and cleanliness is next to godliness. The mantra 'Don't organise other people unless you are organised yourself!' can easily be taken to extremes and can be a constant, consuming diversion. Some people spend their entire careers doing it.

When people offer advice on 'Time Management', the focus is about the aspirations of the person in question and the needs of the people higher up in the organisation - and time is structured accordingly. No wonder the people doing the work feel alienated, unimportant and undervalued.

'Time Management' is big business. There is a preponderance of courses and tutors all earning a living on Managers' inability to organise themselves. It can often be self-defeating: "We know you are bad at managing your time but 'Guess what?', we are going to take up more of your time, telling you something you don't want to hear and something you are not going to be able to practice." They miss the mark – and by a long way. They want Managers to fill their schedules with 'thinking time', 'strategy meetings', 'mind-maps', visits, cold calls, web-browsing, emails and, inevitably, the next Time Management course. With the insistence on 'Urgency', 'Importance', 'Time Robbers', 'Planning' etc., there seems to be a deliberate attempt to omit the quandary that most people face each day: 'What am I here to do?', 'What is my purpose?' and 'What am I trying to achieve?'. There is a significant gap between what people do and how they believe they actually use their time. The problem is compounded: having the wrong impression of the job and not actually fulfilling it. There is no point in organising the day around a perception of a role which could well be flawed and misconstrued.

The difficulty lies in understanding one's true purpose which should then be reinforced by the time demands placed by the organisation. Without any explicit prioritisation, planning and scheduling of the day, the situation can only get worse. With everyday pressures and distractions, the person who has no plan at all has a diary filled with the flotsam of ultimatums from everyone else. There is scant regard to other's priorities – and why should there be? An empty diary is fertile ground for an array of diversions and distractions with varying agendas that never seem to be aligned. Often the Manager is a willing victim and more often than not, it is either self-inflicted or sought after. A person's span of concentration is in complete synchronisation with their interest. In the middle of a desperately dull report, a less than exciting conversation, an altogether familiar task, what is better than a completely unexpected interlude, being interrupted and deflected from the tedium of the task in hand? We are all guilty; we are all complicit in our search for distraction.

There is an obvious hypocrisy here. Employees are asked that they clock in and out on time, that their day has structure, is guided by processes, customer demands and systems. Their days can be measured, their efficiency and productivity monitored and assessed as each 'man hour' and 'man minute' is important in the endless stream of competition and the unrelenting tide of continuous improvement. If each Manager was to establish: 'This is what I am paid to do, this is what I, as a Manager am required to do', how much of that loose puddle of time between starting and finishing is used on the very tasks for which they are responsible and accountable?

Why is this? Why do Managers cast aside the specific and obvious responsibilities in favour of the monotony of meetings, administration and accounting? Have we become lackeys to a bureaucratic machinery that demands attendance at collective séances and compliance to the collation of every piece of

Management data? Why do we hire Managers when the requirement is for clerks?

Don't judge each day by the harvest you reap but by the seeds that you plant. Robert Louis Stevenson

Time spent with people is not something we should be doing 'later' but what needs to be done 'from the start'. Whilst the alarm bells of the inbox and telephone are chiming, a Manager is still required to spend time with the people for whom they are responsible. As such, Time Management is not an 'add-on' – a subject confined to the notes, skills, pastimes and tricks of the trade of other Management epistles. Management of people is not something to be pursued when everything else has been taken care of – firstly, because it never is 'taken care of' and secondly, because that is not the job in hand.

Taking time in the day to discuss options, ideas and the welfare of Employees is the most important activity a Manager can undertake. It is not a question of *not having time* – you can't really afford not to. It takes discipline to make it part of the daily routine because, no matter the circumstances, people always respond to the interest shown in them.

Fortunately, I have experienced events falling into place as though they had been waiting for just the slightest nudge of opportunity (circumstance is like luck – it needs a lot of determination and effort). Some years ago, walking through one of the Distribution halls, I spoke to one of the Operators and asked him how we was doing. "Fine!" came the reply. The tone of voice told me something was wrong so I decided to find out what was troubling him. After some coaxing, he admitted that in fact, he was looking for a new job - something a bit more challenging and in keeping with his own ambitions. If only we had something with more emphasis on the education and certification he wanted? I asked him to do me a favour – to stay on at work for a few more weeks.

We had some ideas and several things fell into place – things we had 'talked' about for weeks and months. We had a small production unit that had a few delapidated saws that produced only about 150,000 pieces every year. We all knew it needed updating and maybe this was the spur? Linking with the local Technical School, we sent the Operator and a handful of colleagues on a specialised course, invested in new equipment and set about a new sales drive. With a new department, better qualified people and a range of customers interested in what we had to offer, we increased our output to three million pieces within eighteen months and signed a range of partnership agreements with some very important customers. We had completely stolen a march on the competition. Just as importantly, we had a team of people who were better trained, engaged and keen to make the business work. The story was of their success, their achievement and their pride in their workplace.

"Delegation is something I leave to others."

What is it about delegation? Is it not just a matter of handing over work to others? Or is it more than that? There has to be, otherwise how can you explain the reticence and prevarication? Is it a lack of trust? Is it easier to do oneself? Is it because Managers are surrounded by incompetent people? The fear of losing authority? Not being involved? Giving away work that is more enjoyable? The loss of knowledge, involvement, respect and power? Or all the above? Whichever way you look at delegation, it should not be done for its own sake -there has to be a purpose.

A man is called selfish not for pursuing his own good but for neglecting his neighbour's. Richard Whately

There are elements of delegation which start with *'can* be done by others' to 'only *I* must do it'. All contain their reasons which are well and truly planted in the collective psyche of the organisation. From the perceived level of competence to the level of secrecy attached to the task; from the time needed to instruct others to the sensitivity the job requires; from the complication of the task to the audience for whom the task is directed. 'If my boss is going to see it, I better do it myself'; 'if I don't do it, it will be taken as a lack of interest'; 'any failure to do the job properly...well, anything could happen!' It is not difficult to see that delegation in its various guises becomes a tightrope. It becomes a recurring series of calculations based on risk factors, available time and interest. It can be expediency, 'it's just better if I do it' or it can be self-importance, "if you want things doing properly..."

There are numerous sides to this coin. I have seen Managers cling to their work as though their life depended on it; I have seen others feel they need to shield their staff from the worst ravages of an autocratic administration. If there are people who are *not* so adept at delegating, there are others who take over the 'difficult bits' for other people in the spirit of management protectiveness. But where does that leave the person for whom the favour is done? Are they likely to get any better? Will they be in better shape to take on other 'difficult bits'? Whatever motives are employed, the outcome is still the same.

The practice of delegation is seen from the wrong perspective. From the untidy and overloaded desk, the rush of priorities, the need to create space and time, the restriction of working hours and the engagements and commitments that can't be fulfilled, it becomes an egocentric exercise rather than one of development and the interests of the individual. 'I am too busy therefore I need to offload', rather than, 'this needs to be done by someone who needs a greater challenge'. It spirals into an exercise in available time and competence rather than a pursuit of personal needs and improvement. Is there a need to delegate because there is too much to do or is it because it is a deliberate step in a person's development? Idealistically it should always be the latter but the former should never be off-limits. Regardless, if Employees believe they are being fobbed-off with the overspill of the in-tray, it is not likely to be given the same care and attention a Manager would like. If Employees understand that it is a way of proving themselves, of reaching the next stage of their agreed development, the task becomes much easier and more rewarding. With this in mind, delegation is not a discipline, it is a *responsibility*. Delegation should be an imperative and an absolute. More time should be given to delegation and the required coaching than anything else. And by doing so, it becomes much more interesting and gratifying.

"Of course we don't like Change, it's in our DNA."

If you know where you are, the directions are numerous and there are no limits to the extent of the journey. Yet, there are big 'conditions' attached. There are prerequisites, there are obligations and there are rules. They are understandable and self-evident but nonetheless need the upmost effort, diligence and discipline. And that is because, if we have to progress, the scenery has to change; the environment has to change; the world has to change and people have to change. 'Change' involves doing things differently; taking a new direction means 'Change' and 'Change' is not something anyone likes doing.

With the results of recent scientific study, we know that the Human Geno shares approximately 96% of its DNA with Chimpanzees and Gorillas. However, our closest relative is the Orang-utan which has lived on this earth for fourteen million years and has a DNA match of 97%. On this evidence, it appears that in this great span of time, our mutual DNA has mutated by just 3%. I do not intend to deduce too much from this fragment of information but nevertheless, this process of evolution serves as a means to illustrate our natural (and inbuilt) nature of keeping things as they are and of *not* changing and preserving our existing 'circumstances'. Our DNA does not like change – in fact it loathes change and any mutation takes hundreds and thousands of years to become apparent. Furthermore, the transference of code from one generation to the next is so accurate it would make any quality professional weep when stacked against their own measures and indicators.

It is, I believe, a question worth posing: why would it be natural for our whole biological structure to be naturally change resistant and yet presume that this circumstance would have no effect on our own free and liberal minds? Observation tells me that there just might be a natural corollary; experience makes me wonder why we should ever suppose we are adaptable, changeable creatures that have much more interest in shrugging off the bonds of nature in order to advance fearlessly towards a brave new world. Our heritage (our nature) comes to the fore for the sake of our species and to ensure there is consistency and continuity. Our natural disposition comes to the fore when there is a proposition to transform the way we do things. Unless it is a pressing inconvenience, we have a natural inclination to keep things as they are – and especially so in the workplace. We are extremely change resistant – literally and biologically. *We* should not be surprised when we resist change. Our natural inclination, as well as our genetic chemistry, is to try to keep things in perpetuity. In fact, the next time you hear that 'Change' is in our DNA – well it isn't.

The fact is, we do things in common and we replicate others' behaviour even if we do not understand why; we follow patterns and cycles of activities whether consciously or unconsciously; we stay with the crowd and we steer away from the controversial; we mimic, we copy and we 'play the game' as others have prescribed. We have our ways of working and our way of doing things; we like to speak to the same group of people; eat the same for lunch and park our cars in the very same place. Often we ask the same questions and have the same conversations. When things are changed, our normal response is to feel uncomfortable and irritated. We resist, we resent and we rebel. Our inner conservatism and reactionary instincts rise to the surface.

I am reminded of a particular passage from a book written by Christopher Hitchens interviewing a long-serving clergyman. "You've seen lots of changes", he asks. "Yes" came the reply, "and I've opposed every one of them!" There are some who use the response 'No' even though it is blindingly obvious that something has to change. But 'change' is instinctively dangerous. There are many who want to improve but resistance becomes a reflex response - it is safer and provides time to explore the consequences and understand the potential repercussions.

"People in any organization are always attached to the obsolete - the things that should have worked but did not, the things that once were productive and no longer are." — Peter F. Drucker

At the same time, there are those who want to be more efficient, more effective, more competitive, more productive and more profitable by repeating the very same processes, making the same mistakes and by doing the same things over and over again. People like to repeatedly bang their head against a wall without looking at any alternative. The belief that insanity is best defined as doing the same thing over and over again and expecting different results becomes ever more tangible and real. In truth, there is a rich stream of madness in every organisation in every part of the world.

An animal's ability to roam is defined not just by its nature but the size of its cage. As human beings, naturally prone to complicate issues, we construct bars and barriers often invisible to others. Our imaginations get the better of us and not only are those bars strong and solid, they are millimetres apart, giving only a glimpse of daylight. But how does this human construct materialise and how are these invisible bars fabricated, strengthened and defended? The challenge has always been to recognise the stumbling blocks, both covert and conspicuous, the signals that are transmitted and how they should be interpreted. There is no point in examining the virtues of change if the barriers are still in place and rigorously defended. However, with everyone alert to the barriers, it becomes easier to navigate a path which is both accommodating and has a purpose. There is always a larger opportunity for success once everyone is aware of the impediments that exist - and are likely to be constructed. Once the barriers to change are eradicated, the possibilities are endless.

It would be a mistake to identify those who are the most vociferous and belligerent as the ones who form the greatest opposition. The people who have sworn their allegiance to the flag of the *status quo* tend to be the easiest to deal with - the source of their protestations are transparent and obvious. If only it was *always* that clear and apparent. Some of the greatest advocates of change are not necessarily those that embrace change. It need not be a quiet, passive resistance nor a muted rear-guard action in the face of overwhelming odds. There are many among those who say, "We need to do something about that!" who use all their efforts to making sure nothing happens at all. Some of the best campaigners are not to be ignored. Those who despise change have the same, if not better, entrepreneurial qualities as anyone else. It is just that their energies are used in different ways. They are just as inventive, energetic, quick-witted, insightful and ingenious. They are not, as popularly assumed, dull, slow and uninspired. They echo the character in Giuseppedi Lampedusa's novel 'The Leopard' (Il Gattopardo) who offers the discernible absurdity that: "If we want things to stay as they are, things will have to change".

Before any constructive argument is built, before any supporting action is initiated, the trenches have already been built and the evangelical script of opposition prepared beforehand. They should not be discounted or taken from granted. *A change process should not only be wary of a fifth column but acknowledge that everyone is a fully paid-up member.*

It takes effort and stubbornness to attempt to keep things free from change. Many a good idea has been thrown on the pyre of innovation by using every common excuse as though they were highly original. Conservatism, is expressed in many ways and the expression, "That's a good point" is one of numerous indicators expressing agreement and resistance at the same time. The reasons to maintain the *status quo* are extremely convincing and carry the weight of strong circumstantial evidence. Every argument can be instantly believable if it has the ring of truth.

One such argument is the claim about the organisation's peculiarity and distinctiveness. Everyone believes their Company is 'special' and 'out of the ordinary'. The circumstance, the environment and especially the people – the chemistry of people together – is indeed unique. When that spills into a reason why things can't or shouldn't be done differently, the argument becomes quite different and one that dismisses the imperatives of progression and the urgency of change. To use the peculiarities of the business as a reason not to change is perilous to say the least. Considering each organisation as 'unusual' and 'untouchable' becomes an extra barrier and an added hurdle to doing things differently –and better.

All conservatism is based on the idea that if you leave things alone you leave them as they are. But you do not. If you leave a thing alone you leave it to a torrent of change. G.K. Chesterton

There are two perspectives, dependent on character, experience and the environment: is 'Change' the edge of a cliff or the bottom of a steep slope? Two widely different perceptions present themselves and whilst much attention is given to the former there is comparatively little focus on the latter. The majority would not care to climb the 'hill of change' because there are enough battles to fight on their resident plateaus. If only they knew that by climbing the hill, they would leave many of the trivialities behind (even though that is a hard message to sell). Regardless of any evangelical zeal, it is not a simple matter of switching off one's natural defences. Indeed, the obstacles might well be real and justified; there might be ingrained concerns but there might well be real barriers in place; there might be other priorities and unknown factors. The challenge lies in understanding the starting position, acknowledging the imagined limitations and understanding the real ones. The precariousness of a perceived position sows the seed of doubt and hesitation. It might be fear or it might be lethargy; it might be trepidation or lack of insight.

"Change? Me?"

Asking someone whether they are advocates of change might well bring forth a list of suggestions and successful, home-grown proposals. Asking someone what they have done themselves, and to what extent they have changed their own routines and ways of doing things, may well produce a different reaction entirely. "But I love change" many have told me. Well, we like changing the way things are done by *other people*; we like to see changes when we see other people doing things wrong; we like to see a change in Government when the leading party fails on its promise. We like to see things done differently but not necessarily changes in the way _we_ do things. We do not like surprises, we do not like modifying our habits, our personal preferences or structured rhythms of activity throughout the day and we positively detest imposed alterations. We do not like changes in our own _processes_, our _systems_ (and ways of viewing data), our _responsibilities_ and our _disciplines_. The fact is, we resist the very things that bring about the most substantial changes – and the factors that actually make that change sustainable.

He that leaves nothing to chance will do few things ill, but he will do very few things. Lord Halifax

Those that argue for radical changes in work practices, changes in working hours and shift patterns might well be the same people who would eagerly man the barricades if it meant moving their office to the other side of the corridor. In the tide of sweeping changes, with livelihoods in peril and when survival becomes a serious issue, I have seen grown men and women argue about the placement of their desks, how big the windows should be in their new office and how far they might have to walk to the second photo-copier (in the event the first one is broken!). It becomes petty and pitiful and makes heroes of the people who possess no influence and have to rearrange their own personal time and arrangements without recrimination or argument.

The Reality of Change

From work processes, to new technologies, to new strategies, customer-handling techniques, re-negotiations and organisational structure, the greatest impediment is the ambition of the person in charge. There are those who believe in the 'art of the possible' – a noble and pragmatic point of view you might say but one that betrays the constraints and limitations of those who use it. It is an unassuming device used to steer efforts away from the likelihood of disruption. Of course, doing something different and challenging requires risk – a boldness and sense of purpose that is often at odds with the usual *modus operandi* – but that can be no excuse to keeping to the tried and tested alternatives. The 'art of the possible' has many variations and many interpretations, so much so that the actual possibilities are hidden under the cloak of doing *something*.

Make no little plans. They have no magic to stir men's blood... Make big plans; aim high in hope and work. Daniel Hudson Burnham

When the organisation aspires to build a bridge across a raging stream, there will always be elements that point to a solitary stepping-stone that can be quickly and easily reached. This serves a dual purpose. It is readily conceived as progress and a step in the right direction and more importantly encourages the organisation to think of manageable leaps, whilst rejoicing in the safety of considered pragmatism. Once the new platform is reached, the dream of the bridge disappears and those that imagined what new ground could be reached are given a warming pat on the back and encouraged to keep up the good work. Change inevitably happens but so much more could have been achieved.

And when things do change, those involved will want to alter what was first envisaged. Even though this is sometimes seen as encouraging, it is not always beneficial. The first call to change the work already being done is normally an initial reaction to the difficulty of the change: the added work, the pressure, the unfamilarity and the realisation of what the change might entail. Change is not always given the opportunity to draw its first breath before improvements are requested and demanded. And by subscribing to this sudden burst of enthusisam, the purpose of the change is sometimes lost in trying to find 'an even better way', 'an easier way' and a way that takes 'less time'.

The road of change is awash with its own natural detours, stop signs, diversions and changing objectives, so much so, it is difficult to remain on course. What's the point of changing something that hasn't even been given a chance to prove its worth and when the results first imagined are not allowed the time to come to fruition? You cannot keep on re-planting a flower hoping it will take root. There needs to be an allocation of time where everyone agrees, "this is the way we are doing it – *and it is the only way*".

A stake in the ground is precisely that – a point of reference. By allowing a multitude of people to deliberately uproot the single reference point and move it elsewhere leaves everyone in a state of uncertainty and bewilderment. Surely it is better to implement properly, develop later and take one step at a time!

"Don't tell them it's a secret!"

The challenge to 'change' leaves a greater imperative to communicate - and to communicate openly and honestly. This is often a matter of willingness, time or circumstance. Sometimes the reluctance to communicate changes can be the result of a direct instruction or from confusion around wider dissemination. At times, it is the lack of confidence in the audience or the one giving the message.

"We can't expect people to understand."

"People will never be able to take it on board."

"Can we trust lower Management to present the message properly?"

And the more visionary:

"If we tell them what this is all about, we will have to tell them what else we have in store!"

Is this not a symptom caused by those not proficient in selling change? Is it not just a result of an inability to understand the culture and the way it works? Truth at times flies in the face of our most basic instincts: people like to have hidden agendas, secrets and confidences especially in a culture where information is power and communication is on a "need to know" basis. Change can be the willing victim of "spin" which is not necessarily about telling people what they *want* or *need* to know but simplistically evaluating what people are capable of understanding. The presumption is that any direct message might well be misunderstood or misconstrued. And within that notion, engagement can quite easily be cast aside as the intellect and wherewithal of Employees is brought into question.

I am of the opinion that there is a certain amount of communication that 'materialises' in an organisation. The less official information, the larger the vacuum created – a vacuum quickly filled by gossip, rumours and hearsay. The absence of any direct information leads to a culture of compensatory language desperate to fill the space with its own 'truths'. And, when the truth is hidden, there should be no surprise when there is resistance to change.

Honesty is the best policy; but he who is governed by that maxim is not an honest man. Richard Whately

It is not difficult to find organisations in which there is a façade of scrupulousness, of integrity and righteousness that is both disingenuous and marginalised. 'We respect our people, we treat them well, they are our greatest asset but... we don't tell them what is going on, we will talk to them when we have time, we will listen when we think they have something to say, we will pay them the minimum wage, we will cut their benefits and we will get them to toe the line.'

Throughout any change process, the values of an organisation are tested – and so they should be. The way an organisation thinks and behaves in any change process is a reflection of its true nature and beliefs. Secrets often occur when a necessary 'shake-up' is called for without saying as much – revitalising the Company's values without telling people what those values are; when there is a need to reduce the number of personnel whilst keeping selected individuals for political purposes; when there is a need to save money in areas when there is no apparent deficit and in order to prepare the ground for new strategies and agendas. Quite illogically, people are seen as a threat and not as a source of ideas; of de-stabilisation not security; as millstones, not as a constant source of energy. It is a common absurdity that the very people capable - and needed - to implement changes are the ones that are habitually kept in the dark.

When I am told, 'keep it to yourself', I am always left wondering who on earth I could possibly tell? Are there enclaves of people dying to find out the latest morsel of information? Do we really believe we live in a network of spies? I am not sure whether organisations are filled with conspiracy theorists who believe their strategy will be given away to 'the competition' or that it is filled with those who fear a mass walk-out on the strength of some spurious rumours. I was once told by a colleague that if everyone knew our strategy, the competition would hear about it in minutes – 'and then where would we be?' I suspected that I would have been surprised if our competition didn't already know or at least had guessed. There were few alternatives. Besides, is the competition always able to do a 'right turn' on the basis of what they suddenly found out about *us*?

In every Change process, there are as many hidden agendas as there are number of people involved. In spite of information sessions and commitment meetings, work groups, brainstorming sessions, committees, forums, newsletters, e-mails, etc. there will always be an overriding agenda which is: 'Where do I fit in?' 'What happens to me?', 'How will I be affected?' It is in our nature and though not intended to be unhelpful, it is one that produces unwarranted frustration and exasperation for those who want to implement the change. Whilst there is an expectation that the whole organisation will march into the fray, banners flying and trumpets wailing, these are not always matched by the consideration given to the real limitations, the promises, hopes and fears, the expectations and guarantees that have been offered to individuals most affected. They may very well be hidden and locked away in order not to dampen the fervour, fanaticism and energy of the latest drive. People can deal with a crisis – and for many change *is* a crisis - if they know the objective and realise how they will be affected. In a climate of secrecy, dishonesty and half-truths it is short-sighted and patronising to claim that 'people only hear what they want to'. In reality it is an admission that Employees have seen through the message and have constructed their own version of the truth.

Keeping everything 'under wraps' causes the limitations everyone is keen to avoid; the hidden agenda is always the slowest moving. Whilst some might suggest there are evidential and practical reasons why some subjects should be secret, not enough thought is given to telling Employees *everything* to *engage* them in a dialogue that is beneficial for all; to inform all Employees as though they really are the organisation's great asset and willing partners. What could happen? What could possibly go wrong? At least there would be no surprises. It could well get people talking and lead to even more speculation but at least it would be speculation based on what they know and not what they *don't*. The speed of change could well be accelerated. If the risks are deemed to be too high, then there should be an honest approach to engagement and a halt to the inconsistency of intentions. Integrity and openess may well indeed expose mistakes and conflicts but at least they would be shared.

Regardless of the nature of programmes and initiatives that take a business from one level of performance to another, it will always be about people. Processes, Systems, Responsibilities and Disciplines revolve around, and are entirely dependent on human input (more on this later). Changing everything else but the people – what they *do* - will not cure anything. There is an established elasticity within any business that will bring any change back to how things were to start with. At best there is an altered state of inertia.

The Habit of Change

Change cannot be about 'knee-jerk' reactions to an unexpected set of events. It cannot be a reluctant response to every unexpected occurence. Change cannot be initiated by announcements and mini-projects as feverish moments of activity before everything settles back to normal. Likewise, change cannot be in the mind-set of the minority - those 'in the know' - who have to presuade the majority why it could be a good thing to do things differently. Change has to be habit forming and has to be an integral part of the culture and mentality of Employees throughout the Company.

The only way to pursue Change is to constantly ask the question 'why?' Like a recalcitrant child who is both persistent and irritating, there needs to be a fundamental questioning of *why* things are done, *why* they are done in such a manner and *what* happens if those things cease to happen.

Somewhere on the outskirts of Glasgow I looked out of the office window and noticed the hills darken as the bright sun slipped behind the approaching, thunderous clouds. The heavens opened and a torrent of rain suddenly became a heavy shower of snow. After a wild, wintry flurry, the clouds parted yet again and the sun made another brief appearance. One of the local Managers nodded at the developing changes outside and said, with a knowing sigh, "Well, if you don't like the weather here, just wait a minute."

If you come to a fork in the road, take it. Yogi Berra

Things happen around us. Regardless of our natural circumstance and inclination, the world is in a constant flux. People are either subject to the ebb and flow of the tides, raging rapids or a stagnant pool - or endeavour to strike out in a given direction. Regardless of our biological, survival instincts, we have to move, progress, change and innovate just to keep up with the competition. The benefits of moving forward always outweigh those of staying still. Seeing change is like being on the North Pole where every move forward is a step in the right direction. More to the point, staying still is the *wrong step* – in fact it is is just asking for trouble.

The argument: "there is no point in changing just for the sake of change" is misleading and insincere – it does not necessarily challenge any progress but reveals the comfort felt with the *status quo*. For those that argue that there is no point trying something, the answer has to be: what is the worst that can happen? What is the worst possible outcome? What tragic or devastating event could possible occur? Either the change will appear daunting or, in most cases, will evaporate as an insignificant factor in the everyday stream of occurrences and events.

The Imperative of Challenge

So why do organisations continually fail to meet their own expectations? Their potential? Their standards and values? Possibly, because they fail to see what can be achieved? There are many organisations that are on the verge of great things - the clamour and insistence on stability is an interference that constantly needs to be ignored. The demand for pragmatism should not be confused with 'making do' – that is infectious, dangerous and is the work of the idle and apathetic. Once you have created the 'perfect' organisation in which people are comfortable, change it!

Only the mediocre are always at their best. Jean Giraudoux

Change the way people do things and everything else will change. The pursuit of change, improvement and excellence should not just be self-centred – it should also be for the advancement of others and by achieving this singularity of purpose, it can be a Manager's greatest contribution – and reward.

Earlier, I put forward a clear definition of a Manager's role which was to 'create the conditions for success'. We should go one step further: a Manager's role should be to *continuously* improve the conditions for success for the benefit of the people involved and the organisation as a whole. Creating the conditions might well imply steering an organisation towards a static set of circumstances that are perceived as ideal, to a position of safety and, perhaps, ordinariness. But this should never be the case. Achieving 'world-class' is about behaviours and how they constantly need to change and evolve. It is not about complicated systems, equipment and irrelevant levels of sophistication.

I assumed someone else was going to write the next bit...

Taking Responsibility

Two of the most influential and ubiquitous elements in any organisation are *complacency* and a lack of *discipline*. These two behavioural traits conspire with each other to foster a culture which promotes conservatism, routine and acceptance. They surface and manifest themselves in the lack of challenge: the failure to identify problems in the mistaken belief that creating a successful team is through avoiding situations of possible conflict, discussion and reasoning. Being the best, striving for excellence can be an extremely uncomfortable and challenging process, even though the rewards can be great. The road that leads away from excellence is paved with the cobblestones of mediocrity.

We can fail on the simplest matters. We find ourselves constantly in the minefield of assumptions - and assumptions are still assumptions regardless of whether they turn out to be justified or not. To 'assume' correctly is like flipping a multi-sided coin and having luck on your side. It is more convenient to skip along like a skimming stone, not daring to delve into the murky waters of detail and afraid of being snagged by the tendrils that complicate the simplest matter. I need not repeat the old adage about the word *assume* but there are reasons why people within organisations have to 'assume', have to 'guess', 'suppose' and 'hope'. Some of it is the lack of communication; some of it is giving up on trying to find an answer; some of it is custom and practice; some of it is laziness and complacency. Success and accomplishment soon become accepted as normal and the urge to be better, to be more effective and to improve, evaporates in an atmosphere of contentment. Even in the best organisations, complacency creeps in like an innocuous infection. It befalls any organisation that becomes distracted from its purpose - providing a coherent method of working with others, rather than an expedient framework of position and rank.

The Organisation at work

The best set of conditions occur when the organisation is in a constant movement and synchronised; a society of individuals with their own way of working but in tune with what needs to work. Getting things done without assumption, without supposition and without the broken hope that others are doing their job as they are supposed to.

My brother in law, rather ambitiously, constructed a revolving sun-house. Not being a mechanical engineer, he reasoned that, due to the size and weight of the structure, the motor would have to be extraordinarily large to rotate the house on its axis. Rather than relying on his own estimates, he asked the advice of an expert in all matters of gearing and ratios. It transpired that the motor he was thinking of installing would have been so powerful it would have shredded the gearbox in seconds. 'No', the expert said, 'you only need the smallest amount of power – the gears will do the rest. That's what they are there for!'

It is a compelling metaphor of how an organisation should work. The initiatives taken by one department are immediately reflected in others. The people doing the work help to propel the ideas, actions and decisions to service the business, the process, the products and the end-customer. The person who understands the markets, the challenges, the customers and opportunities only needs to make the slightest turn and the rest of the organisation turns with them. The question of status becomes superfluous. The only matter of importance is whether the cogs add *value* and whether they actively drive the vehicle. They may be turning round but are they just *spinning*?

Leaders frequently announce that: 'we must improve'; 'we must do things better'; 'we need to be more efficient' without recognising the part each wheel and each cog has to play, often regarding them as expendable parts of the machinery. Trying to 'change gear' when all the cogs are not aligned expends a lot of energy but with no purchase they will have little 'bite' and little effect.

The difficulties of Change are not just found in the way individuals respond and react. The root cause of problems are found in the way the organisation is structured, the way it communicates, the way it manages and the way it regards the one essential element within it – their Employees. Any lapse into condescension, disdain and outright arrogance - determined by an archaic view of the hierarchy – will shape and colour the response. The grains of success lie in the internal fabric of any organisation. There is no black science involved; there is no hidden 'cure-all' for all defects. Within the Process, Systems, Responsibilities and the Discipline in carrying out each activity, lie the drivers of improvement and excellence as well as the satisfaction of the Client paying for the products and services.

Trouble averted

Change and Sustainability

Have you ever wondered why external training courses never seem to work and why they never seem to hit the mark? Why trainees, who have received the very best education, are never quite able to implement what has been taught? Why is it that certain initiatives become stuck in the mire of conflicting agendas, priorities and requirements? Why are 'good ideas' embedded in a pile of priorities that never seem to be complete? Why is it that Continuous Improvement strategies become an elusive ambition and each failed enterprise gives birth to a multitude of excuses? Is it the result of pressing issues and problems within the business with no impetus to resolve them? Is it the result of mixed messages and the lack of clarity around the objectives? Is it a lack of compatibility and uncertainty around any declared outcomes?

Maybe there is a different way at looking at the problem. Perhaps there is too much reliance on System data which fails to support the Process? Conceivably, the solutions are process-based without proper regard for the responsibilities of people within their business? Maybe, those who are given responsibility do not possess the right skill-set? Regardless of how the situation is construed, the problem arises when some essential elements of the change process are introduced without regard to the others. People are taught to do things differently without the right Systems and Processes in place; changes in the Processes and Systems are introduced with scant regard to the Disciplines and Responsibilities that are required. There is too much a reliance on the process of change rather than the outcomes; the methodology and governance of change rather than the result.

Ultimately, the fundamental yardstick of any progression is how people *act* differently and what people *do* differently. Re-engineering programmes consistently forget the one element that makes them sustainable and ultimately successful – *a change in behaviours*. This essential ingredient tends to be lost in the paraphernalia of Management-speak, process labels and strict principles of whichever improvement methodology is adopted. By resolving and 're-engineering' just two parts of the business (Processes and Systems) there is a tendency to see them as total solutions. Business Process Improvements are exactly as they are described and form a narrow view of improvement. It is why lasting, sustainable improvement becomes difficult. Change programmes are not successful by the introduction of new systems but by what people do with them and as result of them. Sustainability is not achieved through Processes and Systems but through people. Any change programme cannot be implemented in isolation of the needs of the Company; discipline cannot be expected when people are not clear of their responsibilities; it is difficult to expect responsibility when there is no agreed Process and no agreed System with which to work.

The application of learning is challenging at the best of times and is made even more precarious by the amount of behavioural change required - and the appetite and willingness to adopt that change. Unquestionably, all facets of change need to be looked at in parallel; lessons can only be applied if the environment provides the right conditions and if those conditions are constantly examined and improved. Companies are not made up of individual furrows for each person to reach their intended goals. A Manager might well be able to create a haven of excellence but it will be relentlessly ravaged by the culture, customs and practice that surround it.

If Management is about creating the conditions for success, there needs to be a method by which the conditions are linked and measured. The pivotal, *cornerstones* of change are: The Process, the System, The Roles & Responsibilities and the Skills and Disciplines involved in carrying out each task. By neglecting just one of these, the effectiveness of a change initiative is significantly altered and the likelihood of that change being sustainable, severely limited.

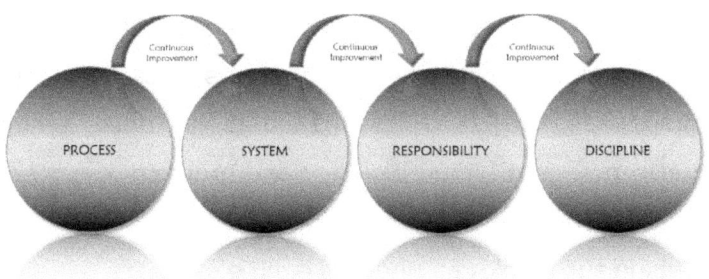

What do each of these 'cornerstones' mean?

PROCESS: The Process is the sequence of tasks, activities, points and transfers of information involved in the delivery of services from beginning to end. In essence, the process answers the question: what service are we providing? It also includes the _process_ of planning, the technical or quality _process_ as well as ancillary support such as maintenance and engineering.

The Process includes: activities or tasks, timescales, lead-times, bottlenecks, points of storage, despatch and delivery to the end-consumer.

This in turn looks at whether:

- Each activity supports the delivery of services to the paying customer.
- Each activity in the process adds value.
- Each activity and sequence is carried out correctly.

SYSTEMS: The data, information and structure specifically designed to support all parts of the process. With a functioning system we can answer the question:

how is the process, organised, measured and how well is the business performing? Systems include; planning guidelines, targets, KPi's, measures (including technical) performance, SLA's, efficiency and productivity, meetings and reports.

This in turn looks at whether each element:
- Supports each part of the process.
- Captures what is happening (in real time).
- Are accurate and timely.
- Is understood.
- Is used.

ROLES & RESPONSIBILITY The ownership and responsibility assigned to people involved in the implementation of the process and the delivery of system support. Roles and responsibilities are encompassed in the organisational structure, the agreed accountabilities and the ownership of each part of the process and the system. In effect, who does what? The simple questions are:
- Does everyone have a role to play?
- Do people know their responsibilities?
- How do they support the process elements?
- How do they use the systems?

DISCIPLINE: The methods, manner, competencies and skills required to carry out all responsibilities to the prescribed standard, consistently - and on time. We may take the responsibility for doing things but how well is it

done – and how often is it done well?
- Are people trained and is skill and capability recognised and rewarded?
- Are the skills and competencies required to carry out each task understood and demonstrated constantly?
- Is everyone able to understand and communicate Company values and objectives?
- Does everyone constructively challenge current practice – and suggest solutions?
- Is achievement and performance recognised?

**Change your thoughts and you change your world.
Norman Vincent Peale**

I did not want to attempt to write an instruction manual but these simple principles on which any organisation should be built are often forgotten in the midst of activities, deadlines and the more interesting technicalities of the change itself. The Process, System, Responsibilities and Disciplines are the basics of any business and are there to be developed and used. It is surprising how often they are neglected. However well the journey is made, it cannot be just dependent on paying attention to each of them in isolation but ensuring they are understood - and how they work in unison. These four foundations form a structured method of identifying and verifying *where you are; where the business is and how the change has progressed.* They shape the key influencing factors in any organisation and are the components that can be changed with wide-reaching significance. They provide any Manager with a structured method of changing the environment and influencing how the organisation performs and improves. Instead of being the victim of these influences, there needs to be a continuous interrogation of: 'What can be changed?' and 'What can be done differently?'

Management – or Managing - is principally the study of responsibilities and disciplines, characteristics that can be fully utilised in a determined way to create the right platform but only *through* and *with* efficient Processes and Systems. There is an obvious starting point: the Process. It should be the origin of any continuous circle of improvement. If a Manager has to create the right conditions, understanding the Process, shedding light on how it works and how it can best be improved is the best way forward.

There is a common assumption that people know what happens in a **Process** from start to finish – from the sales order, to the purchase of materials, to forecasting and planning, meandering through the tributaries of the operation before ultimately finding its way to despatch and delivery. In reality, there are certain people who know their 'bits' of the Process and there is a reliance that it all fits together and 'works'.
Is it possible to change the process without knowing how it all works? Without knowing *how* it all fits together? It

is not really conducive. In fact, mapping out the Process in detail is crucial before instigating any change. It starts to answer a fundamental question that is vital in any organisation – why are certain things done, why are there delays, why is there so much paperwork, why are there inefficiencies and why do people behave as they do?

One of the most important questions any Manager or Supervisor needs to answer is: 'Have we had a good day or not?' The **System** should be the indicator and the arbiter of what constitutes a 'good', a 'mediocre' or, a 'poor' day. If the System works well, it should not be down to 'gut feel', perception or sentiment. There should be shared and agreed parameters of what constitutes 'good' and a measure of any anomaly. The System can so easily fail to measure the points in the Process that need measuring and by so doing, take on a life of its own. As each Company lurches steadily into more advanced digital data-capture system methods, it is not the availability of numbers but the understanding, usage and ownership that becomes the problem. The plethora of KPIs and other assorted metrics does not aid Management of the Process if none are fully understood. Each system should contain all the elements in how the Company forecasts, how the work is planned, how the work is assigned and implemented, how the work is measured and reviewed, how variances are highlighted and how actions are identified, not only as inputs to a new plan but also to *drive* areas of improvement.

And if there are Processes and Systems, there need to be people in place that are responsible. If there is a misalliance in Systems and Processes, it becomes quite obvious that a similar disparity and confusion occurs with people's **Responsibilities**. The boxes in an organisation chart can become arbitrary fixtures based on a perception rather than a real understanding of functional imperatives. Aligning responsibilities with the Process is difficult enough – matching responsibilities with the people who can carry them out can often appear tenuous and dubious. The point being that responsibilities need to mirror - and be aligned with - specific parts of the System that in turn measure specific parts of the Process. It is when organisations become detached from the Process that objectives become divorced from the purpose of the business, that targets conflict and where silos occur. The metaphor of a gearbox is pertinent in how those responsibilities fit together to make the business work and rid the organisation of the obvious and prevalent hierarchical constraints.

When Responsibilities are aligned, the **Skills and Disciplines** have to be applied to make sure that things are done by those who are trained and skilled in providing what is required. Being good at what you do, consistently, reliably and unfailingly is not just an essential requirement of the individual but of the organisation (and thereby the Manager) in providing the conditions by which this can be achieved. Creating the conditions is not only providing the right environment but also providing specific training, development and guidance in how those skills can be mastered. Having responsibility is one thing, making sure those responsibilities add value and provide impetus to the rest of the organisation is quite another. Discipline is not just about capability, it is the consistency of delivery and whether the job is done, as and when required, without fail. Skills are of no use if they are not effectively employed and discipline is of no use if the wherewithal to accomplish the task is overlooked.

The trouble and repetitive conflicts in achieving sustainable change is the reliance on known quantities and the conditions which are achievable with little effort. Yet, there has to be a foundation - there is no point building a house without firm underpinning, without people understanding the service they are providing, without knowing what the Company wants to achieve, without understanding the part they play and to what extent they are accountable and whether they have the necessary skills to carry out their responsibilities. Sometimes we hear the phrase, 'Let's go back to basics' without really understanding what the 'basics' are; when they are too hard to define and the explanation becomes too difficult and complicated. It is like trying to press a magical *reset* button when the button in question is missing. 'Going back to basics' is often a plea to halt the continuing interference and complexity whilst *not* adhering to the fundamentals. Most often it is a cry for change when the continual 'banging of heads against a brick wall' is causing a massive, organisational headache. It is often heard in situations when the organisation is trying to do things *right* without doing the right *things*.

Values before Strategy

Isn't something missing? Is there not something on which any business enterprise and commercial entity should rely? What are the absolute foundations on which a Company rests? What characterises its ethos, its way of doing business and ultimately its culture? What are the guiding principles which steer the governance and well-being of their Employees, servicing end-users, suppliers and the wider community? Many would turn to their Customer Base, their Business Plan their Forecast and their Strategy. But what about Company values? What are the agreed Company standards? How do people in the organisation work together? How much trust and respect is shown for each department and each individual – and how is that demonstrated on the shopfloor, the office and even in the market place?

"Those are my principles, and if you don't like them... well, I have others." - Groucho Marx

There are many aspects of this 'value' conundrum. Some organisations adopt values that are convenient at the time; some turn a blind eye to values that are too compromising and too difficult to implement. Companies very often speak about Company values without really having any. 'Customer Care' might be a respectable value but may well fall short in practice; some have values that are quite blatantly ignored. One manufacturer I knew, systematically - and in their eyes – legitimately, under-delivered to their customers. It was their way of 'compensating' for losses in others parts of the process. Proclaiming values that cannot be kept - or compromising values for profit - are symptomatic of an organisation that has lost its footing. No matter which way we look at it, honesty and respect is not easy to foster and encourage when Employees see blatant dishonesty in the activities in which they are asked to take part. Why try to isolate pockets of deceit in the hope that it does not pervade rest of the Company? How is it possible to respect Employees when consumers and business partners are not respected? How can a culture of honesty be bred when external customers are continuously deceived? How can *trust* be promoted when organisations cheat? How can loyalty be valued when Employees are treated as disposable commodities? How can confidence be engendered when Managers are seen to be disingenuous and hypocritical?

There is no shortage of examples. From the label on the product that has misleading information to the euphemisms in the way 'changes' are implemented in the organisation. When large organisations are brought before a senate or parliamentary committee, do their answers provide a warm feeling of trust and pride in their Employees – or are they seen as political deviations dreamt up by their incumbent spin doctor? Does the literature, the marketing and the promotion articulate the capabilities of the Company or as they seen by Employees as deceitful and impossible to achieve? Are service levels seen as arbitrary indices or heartfelt objectives? When large Corporations state that their profit projections are higher than the previous year but need to make cuts; when Energy and Utility companies use wholesale price rises as a reason to increase the bill but fail to cut them when the same prices fall; when food companies advertise the use of 'all natural ingredients' when they are nothing of the sort; when multi-national companies use loopholes in the tax law to limit the amount they pay in the countries they do business and when Newspapers proclaim their values despite tramping all over them in the pursuit of a good story.

These are convenient and obvious examples. They are the stuff of lawsuits, accusations of mal-practice and corporate hypocrisy. But what about the values that are on the noticeboards, on the walls in the reception areas and canteens? Are they understood and more importantly, are they followed? What do they mean? Are they expressed in a way that is understandable and specific? How can a poster preach 'Honesty', 'Teamwork' and 'Truthfulness' whilst in the same meeting room, something quite different is taking place? How can the words on the poster announce the importance of engagement while at the same time, attendees in the Boardroom secretly discuss the reduction of labour spend? Can any organisation say they have strong values in the Company when everything else – either on an overt or microscopic level - screams something quite different?

One Company I worked with used key-fobs instead of cash for their vending machines. When they decided to raise the cost of hot drinks, they removed the price from the vending machine in the hope that no one would notice. Only on close inspection of the amount remaining on their fob would Employees have realised any discrepancy. Consider their reaction when they realised. Even the shop-floor Supervisors were nonplussed. How can this surreptitious step be taken at the same time as proclaiming engagement, openness and honesty? Yes, it only a small piece of the wider picture but does this make it right, superfluous or unimportant?

Of course it is easy to hide behind the argument of *degrees* – it is only a *bit* dishonest, it is only a *triviality* in the scheme of things, it is only minor collateral damage in a wider strategy. Whatever or however internal and external customers are described, the same values have to be demonstrated consistently and overtly. Values are an essential and critical part of maintaining the integrity and ethics of the Company.

The lack of genuine values in an organisation is pervasive and ultimately costly. If only half of the time spent on strategy was directed to adhering to an agreed set of values, the Company would benefit enormously. Whether they pronounce the absolutes of profit and market share or whether they exemplify the best in terms of humanity, trust, compassion, honesty and integrity, they would form the first step towards consensus and engagement. The values of any Company must be the bedrock – the foundation on which all else it built. It is a set of principles that any organisation should 'hold dear', that are not to be budged, shifted or altered for the sake of pragmatism and the clarion call of *'reality'*. And whilst it is easier, more comfortable and neutral to pin a Company's hopes and future on a strategy, it is the actual *values* of a Company that ultimately defines how it performs.

"Of course we take Lean seriously, we've built a whole department around it."

When organisations feel the need for change, there is a deliberate look at what is on offer in the wider world to drive that change. Rather than making the organisation work as it should, the first point of call is an outside initiative that will allow the business to flourish and prosper; a new idea that will herald a new drive towards improvements; a new strategy that will yield the greatest benefits and keep everyone – the Board, stakeholders and shareholders, happy. And instead of using what is already within their grasp, there is a deliberate directional change that will act as a remedy to all the conceivable ills and create a sustainable revolution. Why not use *Lean* as a new strategy?

Often it is not just about knowing where to go, it is also about avoiding the dead ends, the blind alleys, the cliff edges and the endless tracks that lead nowhere. And yet, so often, organisations are led by labels that have a nice ring of change and sustainability. 'Lean', with its many interpretations and connotations becomes a cure and a lucrative avenue for an eager and enthusiastic Management team.

Nothing is more dangerous than an idea, when you have only one idea. Émile-Auguste Chartier

The reality is that in implementing 'Lean', there should be no surprise when the first consideration is the labour bill and the last item on the agenda is the size of the Company car. When cutting costs is paramount, it becomes a disingenuous 'call to action' when there is investment in new offices, equipment and the expansion in the higher ranks of the organisation. 'Lean' becomes a pretext to cut and skewer slices from the organisation, like salami - a bit *here* a bit *there* - without too many interruptions and conflicting arguments. 'Lean' can easily become a surrogate label to cut costs that should never have been there in the first place.

More commonly, 'Lean' is the natural extension of the

epidemic of 'downsizing' that started in the 1980's and has carried on ever since. And with it, a distinctly unhealthy view of the role of Management and the value of the people in the Company's employment. In *Bright-Sided: How the Relentless Promotion of Positive Thinking Has Undermined America,* Barbara Ehrenreich wrote: "…in the 1980's, came the paroxysm of downsizing, and the very nature of the corporation was thrown into doubt. In what began almost as a fad and quickly matured into an unshakable habit, companies were 'restructuring,' 'reengineering,' and generally cutting as many jobs as possible, white collar as well as blue . . . The *New York Times* captured the new corporate order succinctly in 1987, reporting that it 'eschews loyalty to workers, products, corporate structures, businesses, factories, communities, even the nation. All such allegiances are viewed as expendable under the new rules. With survival at stake, only market leadership, strong profits and a high stock price can be allowed to matter'."

'Lean', it has to be said, sounds more positive, pro-active and dynamic whereas 'cost-cutting' and 'downsizing' sounds like a last resort. 'Lean' becomes a badge – an indication of progress and progressiveness. It becomes an ultimate model, a quintessential ideal with a borrowed set of values. Either it is the fulfilment of a string of customer requirements or a convenient umbrella in which to herd a number of disparate projects. In reality it becomes a policy that tries to eradicate the worst and most excessive costs without any collective purpose. It becomes the new mania that everyone needs to adopt before they are left behind. Simultaneously, in the zeal to trim the fat of the lumbering corporate beast, there comes a whole army of specialists, belted practitioners and automatons, desperate to practice their black art without too much regard to the consequences. Hiring consultants and specialists to cut costs becomes a form of operational blitzkrieg by proxy – a way of implementing swingeing cuts which commonly becomes a short-term misadventure, doomed to short-term benefits.

The rigorous application of labels demonstrates a lack of certainty about the likely outcome and how it needs to be managed. The people who best understand the disciplines of 'Six Sigma' and 'Lean' are those quickest to discard their principles; by knowing them you can be free of them. Someone who picks up the 'Prince 2' handbook at the start of the project is not going to be your best Project Manager. The person who wants to apply the principles of DMAIC to moving a cupboard is going to waste everyone's time.

If there is a need to convince an organisation of a future direction based on a label it is bound to cause scepticism and resistance. Unfortunately, 'Lean' is something that is talked about at Mid-Management to Senior Executive levels for the purpose of Mid Management and Senior Executives. The new religion exalted by the few will never be a success unless it involves everyone. Without everyone's engagement, it becomes a passing phase, a flavour for the season, and a convenient by-word for all that is not fully understood.

I was in a small factory in the Midlands not so long ago. The biggest issue was the amount of spillage and waste. To illustrate this, they mounted a poster on the wall of the smallest, grubbiest canteen I had seen in a long time, crammed with factory operators on barely a living wage. The poster proclaimed the virtues of 'Total Quality' and 'Lean' and to do so, illustrated in graphic detail, the number of BMWs the Company could buy if they added the total disposal bill together. The intended audience would have had to save their entire wage for a year to afford a down-payment. Is this being clever or mindless? Appealing or distinctly off-putting? The intention was well-meant even though sloppy and simplistic and indicative of the 'cut and paste' mentality towards well-meaning doctrines.

The route map to Continuous Improvement is not linear. Management is not a logical, rational process – or profession. Much as rational and researched labels such as 'Lean' are frequently used, they are hollow sentiments and mean little to the individual. We cannot ask the individual to be 'Lean' much as we never ask an individual to adopt the strict disciplines of 'Six Sigma'. We do not introduce TQM into the home or principles of organisational theory in the social club. 'A place for everything and everything in its place' need not be an academic exercise.

When the organisation asks Employees to adopt the principles of 'Lean', what do they mean? Do they want people to be more efficient, more engaging, more responsive and provide yet even better service? Or are they looking for the last buck, the last squeeze of the lemon, the last penny in the march to increase shareholder value and the last drive for efficiency - so they don't have to themselves? The first question to ask when someone mentions 'Lean' is 'why?'

If you don't know where you are going, you might wind up someplace else. Yogi Berra

By examination of the 'core' business – what the business is designed to do - comes a new perspective on what is actually required. And with that, people become more valuable, more intrinsic and more engaged. Before any label is used, the question that should be asked is, 'What does the business need?' To be more efficient? To produce faster? To produce more? To be more collaborative? To be a better place to work? To better serve clients? To meet market demands? To be managed better? When someone next mentions 'Lean', or 'Six Sigma' or anything else for that matter, the question is not only 'why' but 'why can't we do this ourselves?'

Continuous Improvement

A really good group exercise for any Management team is to envision a 'Greenfield site': to imagine a new enterprise, a new building, a new set of Employees, ideas and principles. The rules in this imaginary game are simple: there are no budgetary constraints, no ideas are censured and every suggestion has to be respected. There are a few stipulations: the envisioned factory, office or retail centre needs to supply a quality product, needs to generate income and needs to be a well-respected employer. So, what should a new enterprise include? A new location? A new catchment area? Perhaps an inviting place of work where recruits would arrive with smiling faces in contrast to the ill-disciplined, work-shy rabble that populate the lines and flood the shopfloor? A place of welcome rather than a place of despondency; a place where everyone is involved; an organisation with clear ambitions, clear strategies and a clear idea of what success looks like?

A light appears in the eyes of each member as the imagination bubbles with ideas. New processes, new systems, a completely new structure and ethos are imagined. No more heavy-handed bureaucracy; no more inefficient customs and practices; no more ill-conceived directives and rash ideas concocted from the safety of a back office. The systems would work, the processes would be simple, people would understand each other's roles and responsibilities and would respond to what was needed; fewer mistakes would be made and everyone would be encouraged to receive training and instruction. There would be a new reception area (for all Employees), new signage, new ways of induction, new methods of information and communication; there would be development plans, there would be evaluations, reward schemes and self-governing teams with their own targets, objectives and plans and, and... and the list becomes endless.

It is an enlightening exercise. Especially when the team realise that the ideas that would cause the biggest changes are readily within their grasp. To engage and involve, to make systems work, to treat each other with respect does not need new investment, new buildings and infrastructure or an influx of new blood. It quickly becomes apparent that within the symptoms of disappointment lie the origins of success and accomplishment. What are seen as the greatest obstacles become nothing more than figments of a corporate imagination; the biggest hindrances become the springboard for new initiatives. It becomes evident to everyone in the group that the process, systems, the organisation and the environment have become the harbingers of inertia rather than the vehicles of success.

Our deepest fear is not that we are inadequate. Our deepest fear is that we are powerful beyond measure. It is our light not our darkness that most frightens us. Marianne Williamson

Listing the faults in an organisation is not a difficult exercise but it needs an objective eye and often an ability to filter and combine the most glaring faults into common causes and traits. What is it that we persistently get wrong? Where do we constantly fail? What are our collective faults? The mistakes of one department are magnified by another; the failings in one part of the process multiply elsewhere. This seemingly awkward analysis can spiral into a self-defeating exercise which leaves the organisation bruised and battered with no recourse to medicines or healing surgery. The ability to correct errors comes with a recognition of the how they originate. Athletes do not become better solely by concentrating on the areas at which they excel; students do not become more knowledgeable by revising the subjects they already know. But by turning the proposition on its head, there can be a more constructive platform from which real benefits can emerge.

In one organisation, I compiled a list of shortcomings with the working title: 'We *would be truly great if...*' It didn't take long to write. Many of the conclusions were self-evident and the fact is, no one disagreed with them. They were at once reasonable, self-evident and most importantly well within their capabilities. They were an acknowledgement of what usually went wrong but also a call to do something about it – a trumpet blast to do things *right*. I include the list here as an example:

We could be truly great if:

- We completed tasks on time and as agreed
- We did not find reasons *not* to do things
- We did not spend time finding reasons why things *hadn't* been done
- We did not accept the quickest explanation
- We did not assume *anything*
- We reacted to - and acted on - situations that were unacceptable
- We checked the facts, we checked the data
- We followed up on actions to make sure they were implemented
- We expected compliance to the best way of doing things -at every level, with every task and *all the time*
- We did not accept the *status quo*
- We challenged *everything*
- We did not take things for granted
- We did not sit back and expect others to take the initiative
- We never accepted 'no' as an answer; we never accepted an easy 'yes'.
- We recognised and acknowledged when things went well.
- We *acknowledged* failure, we *rewarded* success
- We met each variance with a remedial action
- We accepted, delivered and took the consequences for every action

- We regarded the people in our organisation as our principal customer
- We attended meetings on time and finished meetings *within* time

There are a number of significant features in this list: not only are they eminently achievable, they can be applied to most organisations – but they are also all *behavioural*. Before anyone mentions that the organisation needs a new IT system, a new piece of equipment or new office to become 'great', it is probably worth reminding everyone that all the behavioural failings will remain and are as likely to be exacerbated as they are to disappear. The principle failures of any organisation are contained within the attitudes, perceptions, routines and ultimately the *behaviours* of the people within it. In equal measure, the attitudes and behaviours are the invaluable building blocks to any great success. If people - and what they do - cause the greatest problems, they are equally the essential ingredients to any improvement and sustained achievement. The recipe for the attainment of greatness is not to avoid the issue with the investment of infrastructure and the peripherals of process improvement but to capture the minds of the Company's greatest resource. Structural change might be seen as a natural remedy but it has the healing power of a sticking plaster – a game of Managerial musical chairs that rarely strikes at the heart of the impediments that cause an organisation to fail. Changing, improving and embedding the behavioural components within any organisation is the essential task of any Manager because behaviours create the 'conditions' by which an organisation stands or falls. The trouble begins when the organisation – and the Managers that hold that organisation together – believe that improvement and change come through everything and anything else.

This world of little consequence

By implementing change throughout the organisation there are inevitable consequences – a transformational ripple that, if not seized upon, rapidly settles as the *status quo* becomes reaffirmed and the original conditions return to the norm. Equally, by not implementing any change at all, there are consequences. Consequence is the resulting condition of any action or inaction. There is a consequence of direct intervention; there is a consequence of leaving things alone; there is a consequence in the manner in which things are done and a consequence in the manner things are neglected; there is a consequence of keeping still, there is a consequence of moving forward; a consequence of success and one for failure.

The failure to act, to communicate, advise and intervene has as much a causal effect as direct intervention or instruction. The impact may be more subtle, less conspicuous and obscured in the thousands of events that occur every minute around us but that is not to say they do not exist. And for a Manager they become starker, more real and more...well, more *consequential*.

Newton's Third Law states that to every action there is an equal and opposite reaction. Taken in the context of human relations this law is clearly inadequate. In organisations, the law goes much further: for every action – and every inaction – there is always a reaction but not always equal and commensurate. Much as any act has an effect, so does any *failure* to act.

'Consequence' is a word normally filled with dread and with connotations of conflict and intimidation. The 'inevitable consequence' becomes a veiled threat rather than an appeal for even-handedness. In reality, it should be the voice of 'fairness', 'righteousness', 'integrity' and 'impartiality'. It is an organisational 'driver' that is misunderstood and misinterpreted. Consequence is inextricably linked with the standards and values of the organisation, the ethical nature by which business is conducted and the relationships with the people the organisation employs.

"When you choose an action, you choose the consequences of that action. When you desire a consequence you had damned well better take the action that would create it." Lois McMaster Bujold

Of course, the issue is not that there is always a consequence, the issue is whether each Manager has some measure of the consequence – and whether the Manager understands and anticipates the nature of that consequence. It can be the measure of a Manager's situational awareness – of observing, interpreting, understanding and influencing all that goes on around them.

The trouble is that whereas *consequence* is an ubiquitous element within any organisation it is more apparent in the lack of any undertaking rather than any overt Management action. In the event of mistakes, wrong-doing, lack of performance, people tend to expect some consequence however mild. The *lack* of management interest is a potent signal to the organisation – a signal that tells everyone that certain actions are allowed, faults are permissible and even incompetence is acceptable. If poor performance is 'acceptable' it simultaneously tells the organisation that good performance is *not* considered to be important - or imperative: 'Why should I make any effort if those that don't, appear to get away with it?' 'Why should I follow the rules if no one else does?' 'Why shouldn't I be allowed to get away with things if others can?'

The lack of consequence is a sizable, dangerous and deflationary element in any organisation or culture. It is one of the woolen, silent brakes that impedes progress and success. The lack of management action is a persuasive prompt to the organisation that delay is *satisfactory*; that inaction is *tolerable* and that ill-discipline is the *norm*. When a person walks onto a construction site without a safety helmet and not a word is said; someone is off ill for a number of days and no speaks to them on their return; another books in the wrong numbers into the stock records and people shrug their shoulders; one of the team leaves the production line for a cigarette – against Company rules - and people turn a blind eye. Every action is governed by a mini risk-assessment based on this understanding of Company rules and Company integrity. And when the risk becomes negligible - 'Nothing happened last time I didn't do the job - no one said anything, why should they now?' it should be no surprise that it becomes legitimised and accepted.

By *not* confronting the issue, there is a loud message of collusion and acceptance. By leaving it 'this time', until it is 'more convenient' or more 'pressing', by ignoring it or turning a blind eye, tacit approval is granted which proclaims: 'this is ok', 'this is not an issue' and 'this is tolerable'. One thing is certain – it *is* noticed and registered. It is observed and deciphered by a silent audience and is interpreted as an important reference point about how the team, the department and organisation work. The dangerous conclusion is that parts of the common values within the Company are important, whilst others are not.

This is how cultures work, exist and are founded. People act in ways that are directly linked to what they observe, what they understand and what they perceive. Silence on issues can be just as loud and informative as a detailed explanation. Communication and silence can be equally demonstrative and educational to the individual and the collective culture. We cannot be detached - the constant tidal surges of events, predicaments and instructions together with the perpetual rule-bending, short-cuts, ill-discipline and inactivity act as single-point lessons in how to behave, how to survive and 'get on'. The daily interruptions, demands, expectations, changes of plan, change of direction and mixed messages cannot be ignored and act as living, breathing workshops on how a business needs to be run. They are as instructive and memorable as Managerial coaching sessions.

Talking to one Senior Manager who complained that no one did anything on time, I asked him: 'What happens when people fail to deliver on agreements? What is the consequence?' 'Well, nothing,' he said. 'I just have to accept they were doing other things'. It easily becomes an acceptable state of affairs as the organisation becomes infected with a collective conspiracy of inertia: 'If you don't say anything, I won't say anything and we'll keep quiet about the whole thing and act as though nothing happened!' What do you do? Do you say that it is reasonable to 'leave it a few days' or tell others, 'don't worry about it'? Do you question whether the deadline was too ambitious? Empathise and convince yourself that the person doing the work is possibly 'snowed under' and has other tasks to complete? Once targets are not met – and nothing is said, the task adopts a quite different complexion. The unwillingness to engage Employees becomes translated into mollification and prevarication becomes confused with a desire to be more humanistic and friendly. The willingness to become more approachable and likable becomes blurred with the requirements of the job. When it comes to a head, the natural reflex is to encounter the person rather than the problem – and by doing so, create an unpleasant and less conducive atmosphere. The environment actually becomes more confused, more stifled and prone to disengagement.

Managers can often become too *accommodating* in a way that brings the organisation to a 'comfortable' level of mediocrity. The organisation becomes acclimatised to inertia whilst ambitions are adjusted to ensure no one is seen to be abrasive and provocative. The trouble is, nothing great has ever been achieved from a situation of comfort; no great standards have been achieved by accepting second best; no great obstacles have been overcome by skirting issues and jumping at the point where the bar is lowest. Too often, in the face of disaster, it is uncomfortable to question the avoidability of the dilemma and instead, rush to distance the problem and not tackle the issue at all. There is a strength in recognising mistakes; people as well as organisations become stronger by making and recognising them. Breeding a culture of acceptance is the sin of the unambitious and the disillusioned.

On the other hand, confronting the problem immediately

can be perceived as an exercise in conflict – as a form of antagonism and assertiveness. It should be quite the opposite. The fact that the Project Plan, for example, is a day late - and that it has been acknowledged - is a strong indication of the seriousness of the exercise and the importance of the deadline. It is a commanding expression of the values within the Company and that 'professionalism' and 'delivery' are not just by-words in a stream of Management-speak. It sends an unequivocal message that the task is significant and that it needs to be completed. Just as importantly, that there is a willingness to support, encourage and to ensure things are done better the next time. These situations are always potentially uncomfortable as they all raise questions, not just about the practicalities of completing a task but also about the Manager's judgement in assigning the job in the first place.

Sow an act and you reap a habit. Sow a habit and you reap a character. Sow a character and you reap a destiny. Charles Reade.

'Consequential Management' carries with it responsibilities, imperatives and values. It contains the very basics of the Management role: the creation of better conditions, engaging people and encouraging them to achieve more and better things. 'Confrontation', in its wider, more positive sense, is a situation to be embraced rather than one to be avoided. It is the doorway and opportunity to ask the question: why was the task delayed, why did we not perform to our best? What were the impediments? What happened? Was it pressure, was it lack of awareness, forgetfulness, lack of experience, training or lack of confidence? The immediacy of any action or message makes it much more understandable and unambiguous - and is much less likely to be tainted by conjecture and perception. Problems and failure are the doorways to Management intervention and a path for every Manager to take at every opportunity. They are the first point of call in the identification and resolution of problems, continuous improvement and individual development.

So what if the plan had been completed on schedule or ahead of time? What if the plan had been meticulously considered and delivered beyond people's expectations? Speaking to a Team Leader on the production lines in a manufacturing Company, I was told how they had managed to identify and 'weed out' the bad performers, the slackers, the dispirited and the uninterested. I had to ask, "Well then, how do you identify those who are doing a great job and what do you say to them?" "Well, we don't do that", came the sheepish reply. "It's not something we are very good at here."

If there is an identification of failure to meet targets, there needs to be an equal and immediate recognition of success. To do one without the other creates an imbalance and a pervading feeling of unfairness, indifference and a lack of trust. In some circumstances, those who do recognise achievement unfortunately have a tendency to praise the person who gets the Company out of the mess it shouldn't have found itself in the first place. It is wrong to judge the effectiveness of an organisation on its ability to get out of the trouble it has caused. This may be a measure of its resilience but not its ability to improve.

The Educational Imperative

"This is not a high school…"

There are differing opinions about the responsibility a Company has towards educating its Employees. Let's face it, Employees are paid to do a job of work and not to spend time in the confines of a training room. Work needs to be done during normal hours and education in *their* own free time. "If they want education, they can go to night school", I remember hearing. "This is a business, not a High School!" I was told by one Director. Well, actually any organisation, large or small *is* a high school. Any business, any organisation becomes a study in anthropology which not only includes social interaction and behaviour but also people's morals, values and beliefs. In reality, everyone in the organisation is being trained every single day in *what* to do and what *not* to do.

Though hardly noticeable, a curriculum is repetitively indoctrinated through how others behave so that everyone in the organisation receives an education of one kind or another. To believe that Employees are only schooled when on a course is to believe that children only find out about life from their parents. 'Best practice' is substituted by 'ways and means', of 'short-cuts', and 'what we can get away with', 'what to report' and 'what to keep hidden', 'when to keep your head down' and 'when to speak out', the 'tricks' to keep the machines running through busy times and how to 'report' events to avoid rebuke.

The aim of education is the knowledge not of facts but values. William Ralph Inge

It is difficult to find anyone who really takes cognisance of this perpetual, internalised education system; this constant application of informal learning which becomes embedded, sanctioned and reinforced. In the absence of anything else, even newly promoted Employees become receptacles of bad practice, inefficient processes, insufficient systems and ineffectual leadership. Even Managers ultimately become limited by the organisation they are hired to improve. Managers adopt the same customs and practices of those they have replaced even if their predecessor's removal was due to incompetence. Each new appointee becomes a student of accepted custom and routine, rather than the vehicle of innovation.

So, how are the conditions shaped? How can Continuous Improvement best be implemented and encouraged? When those in charge see improvements and changes as initiatives that need to be imposed and when the immediacy and convenience of mandatory impositions takes over the long term benefits, problems are bound to occur. The short term expediency becomes a repetitive exercise of brow-beating, frustration and infuriation. How much better, and easier, it would be to implement change when those most affected become the instigators. However, this does not happen by itself and whilst this is a statement of the obvious, it seems strange that this approach is either ignored, treated with enormous amounts of complacency or ditched in the fleeting rush of expediency and haste. If 'Continuous Improvement', engagement, empowerment and adoption of change is the question, then the answer is surely education.

A quick scan of any dictionary will convey the definition of training as *'the acquisition of knowledge, skills and competencies to do a job'*. Regardless, education through training is seen in many different ways by different organisations. It is deemed as both essential and wasteful, intrinsic and irrelevant, vital and neglected in equal measure.

Education makes a people easy to lead but difficult to drive; easy to govern, but impossible to enslave. Lord Brougham

When asked directly, no one would doubt that there is a requirement to constantly develop Employees; no sane Manager would openly state that Employees' development is not their responsibility. And yet, despite these accepted imperatives, in practice it is hard to find evidence this is given any precedence. Those in authority may well consider training and development as one of their most important tasks – it just never ends up that way. Training and development of people is consistently the one activity that is neglected and is often the activity that is left to others. The delivery of personnel development never seems to transpire in a considered and sustainable manner. It is the one activity that comes last in the rankings of how Managers spend their time and it is the one task for which they feel the most guilty for not having done enough. It is the highest priority that never seems to be achieved. This is not only due to the appropriation of time but also a fundamental misapprehension surrounding training and education.

There are a number of anomalies and contradictions that never seem to be clarified and resolved. Some of it lies in the attitude towards training; some of it is wrapped in the constraints and immediacy of the day, the workload and the absolute requirements of a demanding consumer; some is contained within the apparent payback of individual development and a lot of it is grounded in the efficacy of current training practice.

In spite of this, there is a strange divide. The need for *internal* training is neglected in the tide of events, priorities, resources and management availability. When the training is *external*, all manner of options appear. External training involves the least amount of work and is something in which a Manager needs not be involved –

it just something to which people are *sent*. Regrettably, by doing this, a blind eye is turned to its effectiveness and practicality.

"I know, let's send them on a course!"

Of course, it would be convenient to argue that organisations don't invest in people at all, but of course they do – especially with the growth of externally-led 'development' programmes. The trouble is that the courses are primarily for Supervisors and Managers, not the people doing the work. The situation is, admittedly, more confused by the fact that the Managers and Supervisors are sent on courses *at the same time* they are supposedly fulfilling the role - and not *before*. To the objective commentator this seems illogical. Why hire someone to be a Manager in order to illuminate their failings which can then be remedied by going on a course? I don't believe many other professions would be so accommodating.

There are indeed organisations who take training to a different level and have budgets and departments which deliberately (and at times) excessively send people on courses. The trouble is, Supervisors and Managers are sent on training programmes not just as an option but as the *only* option. More training courses, programmes and modules are being established and if there are organisations that are reticent, there are just as many that throw pots of money at training programmes, teambuilding exercises, as well as self-development and personal tuition courses. More aspiring leaders are being pushed through seminars, courses, modules and skills programmes than ever before. But do they work? What is the intended outcome? Is there a tangible change in Managerial competence and capability? What are they trained in? Who plans, organises and delivers the training and what are their motives?

One must learn by doing the thing; though you think you know it, you have no certainty until you try. Sophocles

There are a number of factors here: the driving ambition of a HR department to send as many as possible through a pre-determined education programme; the ready availability of training options and the availability of a budget that needs spending; the expediency of quick and easy learning and the desire to be seen to be doing something! Either way it becomes a dispassionate exercise. Training departments are established with the purpose of getting people through a certification process like a nervous flock of sheep running through a turnstile. The chances of any external training being worthwhile is extremely limited.

The fact is that hard-earned budgets are thrown at courses (and training organisations) with little intrinsic value or merit. Usually, there is a ready-made shopping list of training options that Managers and Supervisors are obliged to attend which are more likely aligned with the contents of a Management textbook than any realistic need. They include a mixture of 'what is available', 'would like to attend' (written down from people's Personal Review) or a perceived theme which tends to crop up though 'Disciplinaries' and 'Exit Interviews'. I have seen solitary Technicians recommended for a Coaching course; Supervisors are sent on a Root-Cause Analysis programme with little evidence of any data capture system and Motivational courses for people with no one to manage.

External *Management* training courses have different ways of being assessed even though the content was 'interesting', the trainer 'amusing' and the facilities 'amazing'. The issue here is the level of expectation. Organisations send people on courses with little anticipation that the student comes back with a new vision of the world, new sets of tools and techniques and more importantly, little in the way of behavioural change.

As a result, when Managers return from expensive courses, the exercise is seen as a waste of money. And in fairness, this may be an extremely reasonable conclusion. There are far too many training programmes that haven't matched the needs of the trainees - or the business - and have been hastily pre-packed and bundled in ways that reflects minimising expenditure rather than effective gains. In every organisation there is at least one thick training folder, doing nothing else but taking up valuable space and attracting every free-floating microbe of dust.

The amount of money spent is really quite staggering. Millions of pounds are spent on off-site training programmes, in stultifying conference rooms with a conveyor belt of coffees and biscuits desperately trying to maintain sugar levels whilst the attendees drift off into a world of their own. There is a distant hope that once a Manager has been through a set of pre-determined modules, he or she should be suitably and adequately trained and that they should be able to cope with most, if not all, the demands of a person in charge. At best, there is a conviction that people have been provided with the necessary fundamentals in Management skills and should find them at least useful. There is a collective understanding that most of these lessons, if not applied, may be remembered and could perhaps serve as a timeless toolkit that will enable all participants to become better and more effective - eventually. Bearing in mind that the sessions are not meant to last more than a few hours, it is a large *ask* and actually one that is unachievable.

In reality, the larger organisations spend a lot of time and effort to ensure the people in the organisation attend the course but spend very little time assessing whether anything was learnt. Still less in seeing anything worthwhile implemented. There is a complete absence of thinking here. There is little real hope of a reinvigorated and enthusiastic trainee and little enthusiasm from trainees themselves that something important will be gleaned; there is little in the way of setting expectations beforehand and little follow up on their return. Certainly, if nothing fruitful transpires, it is easier to blame the course and the pupil. It is a mad merry-go-round of HR driven initiatives appeasing those who profit and those who should know better. If the same diligence used to hire new people was spent on the courses people needed to attend, there would be a considerable change in their effectiveness and the resources used to make those courses work.

Education is an admirable thing, but it is well to remember from time to time that nothing that is worth knowing can be taught. Oscar Wilde.

Quite another problem with Management development is the plethora of Management Trainers and Management programmes that take the *least* amount of time in understanding Managers' predicament and spend *all* their time telling them all they know. When administrators identify a training needs, it is often the case that the interests of the Employee is subjugated to accommodate the subject and interests of the Trainer. What they actually *need* to know and what the trainer believes he or she *needs* to tell them can be two completely different things. As a result, outsiders are brought in with nothing but a generalist knowledge of the subject and no understanding of the conditions in which the trainee has to contend. A 'Time Management' course given without understanding the environment in which they Manage is optimistic but useless, appealing but impractical. A Motivation course given without understanding the culture, pressures and restrictions with which a Supervisor or Manager has to contend is both unhelpful and confusing. The ability to apply the lessons should not be seen as a bonus – a random by-product of a visual and verbal onslaught - it should be the objective and structured outcome. If Management Trainers were only paid on the proven application of their lessons, many would go penniless.

Of course, it would be in everyone's interest if training was based on its pertinence and usefulness; that each lesson could be applied and prove effective. Unfortunately, there is a misalignment between investment and actual gain. For all that is spent in time and effort, there is little tangible evidence that anything has 'improved'. Apart from isolated islands of excellence, there is little interest to determine whether training has had any effect on routines, disciplines and behaviours. Although efforts and investment are commendable, the fact remains that many businesses struggle to assimilate new learnings new skills and new approaches. Talent is there to be developed but this can only realistically be achieved given the right direction.

Our greatest asset?

Coming back to my earlier point, how are the funds divided between the hourly-paid and the Management ranks? Are we not back to same conundrum: that the investment for those who need to take charge and to govern takes precedence over those actually doing the work? That the needs of those who administer are far greater than those who actually add value to the products and services the Company sells? What are organisations actually willing to spend, per Employee on education and training? What is actually contained in the budget as an allocation towards training that amply reflects that their people are their greatest asset? Are organisations prepared to spend more per person than the service costs of a photocopier? There can be an underlying aversion to spending money on what could be singularly advantageous to a Company's Employees but which might not have an immediate and tangible effect on the Company. They are uncertain of what they are going to get. The common impediments to education are the tangible drawbacks stacked against the precarious benefits. It does take a giant leap of faith that Employees in general, given the right conditions and the right investment, will pay them back.

Whilst there are some organisations with loose purse strings, there are others that are more circumspect, especially in the provision of training for the lower levels in the organisation. There is a more thorough interrogation of what is on offer. Can we spare the individual at this moment in time? Will the training programme provide any measurable result in the short term? What's the financial benefit? The more prudent believe that an education programme requires a certain certainty of investment and even a minimum fee needs to be justified through a traceable economic advantage. The immediate needs of the Company can easily outweigh the long term needs of the Employees. This may be symptomatic of either having low expectations of people or the training.

There is another side to these differing approaches and other factors come into play. For a Manager that is unsure of him or herself and has little self-confidence, it takes courage to send Employees on a course and arm them with knowledge that has the potential to unseat their hard-won position. What if they start asking difficult questions – and even more frightening, have the right answers? Suddenly it is them that have all the bright ideas, all the solutions and receive all the favourable attention. Young hopefuls might begin to challenge their ideas, strategies and objectives that have been in place for decades and formed the backbone of their own Management philosophy and know-how. The glaring imperative of education can be lost in the mist of uncertainty and doubt in one's own position.

Nevertheless, the ceiling for what people can achieve should not be defined by the skill and ambition of the incumbent Manager. When stumbling across entire departments that have not been sent on training courses, you can almost bet that the person in charge has also been largely self-taught. The problem, of course, is that the world moves on, and the skill levels deemed adequate years ago are not necessarily sufficient today. True, when money and resources are scarce, one of the first things that fly out of the window is budgetary expenditure on training and development; when production schedules are tight and deadlines are approaching it *appears* to be folly to send people away.

Continuous improvement – of the individual.

I am not arguing that education is almost always wasteful – especially when it comes to Management skills. This would be self-defeating and at odds with everything else I have written. There is no substitute for education but it needs to be 'good' education. Management development through experience alone is like asking someone to put a car engine together: without guidance or instruction they will learn the mechanics of assembly but will never get the engine to work. At best, the Manager will learn the basics through the habits and practices of others. There is no substitute for *effective* training in whatever format or disguise. And if organisations leave Employees at any level to pick things up, they are abandoning them to a career of underachievement and little progress. An organisation is in trouble when there is a heavy reliance on people being *good* at what they know rather than people *knowing* what is good.

So, how should the fundamental task of developing their key resource be tackled? What and whose objectives should be addressed? Are people sent on training courses to develop their skills and qualifications that *the organisation* believes they should have or the skills and qualifications they feel they *need*? Does it suit *the business* needs or *their* needs? Is it in pursuance of what the Manager believes they *should* know, what they *need* to know or what Employees *want* to know?

That is the difference between good teachers and great teachers: good teachers make the best of a pupil's means: great teachers foresee a pupil's ends. Maria Callas

The key to any successful training is to fully understand the person who is to receive the training; to recognise their ambitions and purpose as much as the purpose of the organisation. The individual might very well need to go through certain specified courses but a balance needs to be struck: between aligning and targeting the things that are essential for the organisation and the things that inspire the individual. Is it not more important to consider a more detailed, personal approach to the aims and aspirations of each individual? The 'off-the-shelf' teaching may well be aligned with the exact needs of the individual and their ambitions – but this is less than likely. The important ingredient – as with most things – is the dialogue that leads to the right conclusion and the best outcome for the individual.

Any forum by which a trainee can question facets of their employment, their way of doing things and the questionable normality of their employment has to be a good thing, regardless of the subject matter. If nothing else, a training course, properly presented, properly funded, properly prepared and scripted, allows a breath of fresh air in the certitude of common routine, custom and habit. However much an organisation should endear itself to the ethos of learning, it should not necessarily embrace the apparatus and institutions of learning. Some of the best training programmes can be the impromptu internal sessions based on immediate need. Not only can the real issues be dealt with but the results can be agreed and implemented within minutes of the session ending.

Organisations – and Managers in particular – display a strange sense of humility in not recognising internal training as being much more practical and effective. Training does not need to be seen as an 'away-day' in a far off classroom but time spent in the department, in the office or on the shopfloor with nothing more than a new perspective and a different way of doing things. Training is not about the instructor having the all right answers but asking the right questions. It doesn't need to be planned and well-defined but it needs to be consistent and part of the routine. Ultimately, there has to be an objective - and an outcome if nothing more than the engagement of Employees and the willingness to show an interest in each person's development.

The benefits in training are not just about individual development but also that people reciprocate in kind. The level of interest shown in the individual determines the individual's interest in the Company. This investment need not be seen as a purely altruistic exercise – and there is no reason why it should be. Even our most generous actions towards another individual, given any circumstance, should take our own reward and benefits into consideration. Indeed, taking them into account should never be a reason to ignore them. Neither should the significant benefit for an individual. Is there anything wrong in taking a highly motivated employee and sending them on a communication course because they have had issues with explaining new ideas to their colleagues? Is it wrong to find courses on mental and physical health programmes? Is it wrong to send people through counselling because they have suffered trauma and personal loss? Especially if it means they can become more engaged, more productive and have less time off work?
From specific development plans to social skills; from self-help courses to improving a person's quality of life; from basic reading and writing courses to more advanced technical skills and capabilities there are few things more

rewarding than being a successful person's 'sponsor' and guide.

Even when education results in a person leaving to seek new pastures and avenues for their new-found potential this should not be viewed as a particularly bad thing or a waste. Employees may be a Company's greatest asset but this is not to believe they should all be handcuffed and chained to their places of work. What is a greater advertisement for a Company: 'I had to leave because there were no possibilities of advancement' *or* 'They are a great place to work, they gave me every opportunity to develop'?

The drive towards education, training and personnel development is littered with good intentions. The trouble is that Managers have to invest the time and effort to accomplish this simple discipline and pressing imperative. The importance of developing each Employee at any level should not be relegated to the usual 'tick-box' exercise. Being skilled, capable and competent should not be an assumption based on time served and having learnt the ropes from other dubious sources; it should not be the assimilation of acceptable routines and the application of pragmatic ways and means. To accomplish this, each Manager should take several steps away from the situation and assess what training has already been given and what has been the net effect. Every Manager should assess each activity and each process within their area of responsibility and question whether each person involved has received an adequate level of training and support. Every Manager should ask whether they have personally received sufficient training to fulfil their own role and create the right conditions for others.

Where does this all lead?

"Wait until I find the guy who started this blame culture!"

Does the environment shape the organisation or the organisation shape the environment? Does the organisation shape the Manager or does the Manager shape the organisation? Does the Manager shape the people or do people shape the Manager? Do Employees shape the culture or does the culture shape Employees?

It is extremely difficult to fully comprehend the importance of the conscious and unconscious signals each one of us sends every minute when in the presence of others. This is not always due to exceptional humility but rather a case of limited awareness. People's eyes and ears are remarkable radars of encouragement and threats, opportunities and risk. It is known whether there is good or bad news in the offing before anyone has opened their mouth. Even the most unobservant understand and capture more than they give themselves credit. All elements of seeing, hearing, feeling and touching feed into the melting pot of each other's considerations, beliefs and actions. We are acutely adept social animals, extremely aware of our pack instincts and curious to every anomaly. From this, people determine their behaviours - from people's behaviours, organisations derive their 'Culture'.

The Culture in any organisation is the DNA of that organisation – you can't see it and you can't feel it and is near damn impossible to explain. When asked to describe the culture in the organisation, the one-word answers ('conservative', 'friendly', 'laid-back', 'feudal' and 'awful') are always inadequate. No organisation exists without its own unique, branded culture. It is the root of all that is successful within a business and all that is harmful. It is the Company's lifeblood and bedrock; it is the organisation's best communicator and every single neuron receives the message sooner rather than later. It is easy to feel the victim of all its failings and it takes great understanding and persistence to change. By ignoring it, the Manager will forever be the recipient of all its ills; by keeping some distance, a Manager will never be able to influence or shape its course.

The subject of 'culture' is ridden with presumptions involving environmental considerations, the psychology of the individual, tribal patterns and groupings, verbal and non-verbal communications and an infinite range of variables. It is man's nature to question how we relate to one another (or how we don't) how we interact (or don't), our purpose, ambitions and aspirations, our sense of self, our individualistic or group motives, our age, our background, our influences and beliefs. It is all relevant, it is all stimulating and it is all illuminating. Let's face it, how is it possible to disregard a subject that pervades, informs and dictates the way individuals, groups and organisations work? None of it can be dismissed. But it is not always as overt. People's understanding of behaviour lies as much in an explicit gesture as the slightest change in expression. It is based on familiarity and understanding, customs and conventions, traditions and general practices. Talking to a Manager some years ago, he complimented me on my understanding of how people worked: "Stay a while longer" he said, "and you may understand the sub-culture." "But", he said, teasingly, "you will never know what really makes this place *tick*." He was right, I wouldn't be there long enough. I would not be there to comprehend every knowing 'wink', 'nod', 'shake of the head', 'grunt' and 'silence' that would have as rich a sense of purpose as a fully-fledged mission statement.

'It's the culture here, it's always been like that' has become a recurrent mantra and says more about the messenger it as it does about the subject matter. Culture is believed to be something that 'happens' to us. One can easily become victim to the raging sea over which no one has control. If that was the truth, everyone should throw their hands up and carry on with their day-jobs believing everything was a lottery of events. The reality is that Employees, Staff, Supervisors, Managers and Directors are as part of the Culture as anything else. The victims are in fact all instigators and whilst some are the ringleaders, everyone is part of the entertainment, consciously or unconsciously, willingly or unwillingly. One of the problems with culture is that people see it as a swimming pool into which you can dip your toes but nothing else. Organisations are perceived as 'them' and not 'us', whilst in fact the culture is and has always been 'us' and not 'others'. Everyone plays their own little part: associates, members and initiators on a stage, improvising within agreed but unspoken conventions. As a result, those responsible have to reflect not just on others' behaviour but what their own behaviours cause other people to do. They cannot be frustrated by rumours when they, themselves, are eager to impart the latest gossip; they cannot bemoan the lack of respect when they turn up late to a meeting and decry others attempts at discipline; they cannot blame people's lack of initiative when they inhibit, intimidate and 'micro-manage'.

To use another metaphor, the Culture is the heart and lungs of any business. It sucks everything in and expels it out in ways that are either recognisable or imperceptible. The Culture is the culmination and apogee of so many of the factors that have been discussed previously. The Culture is made up of the organisation's attitude to people, how they are paid, how they are rewarded, how they are 'Managed' and any efforts that are made to measure and *control* them; it made up of how people's time is spent; it is the result of how people are motivated or left to their own devices; it is made up of the consequence of action or inaction; it is the result of any change – or stability; it is made up of the simple acts of communication and how people feel they are engaged and involved; it is the culmination of training and development. It is made up of a myriad of elements some of which are immediately actionable and some which take more time and effort.

It is often seen as a mixture of the true 'essence' of the Company and a curse; a pervading ailment or benefit that is bestowed on the organisation from an unknown source, rearing its head in different ways in each and every department. Very simply, Culture is what people 'do'. Culture is ultimately about behaviour; Culture is about actions, interactions and conduct; Culture is how people respond to situations and how they react to others. Every action is traceable; every action has a reason; everyone's behaviour is a consequence and not a cause.

Given this, the truth of course, is that the Culture can be changed – changed by the mix of ingredients which are themselves alterable, movable and variable. And if the culture does indeed need changing, it demands a thorough assessment of what parts are essential for a Manager to change – and the parts that are left well alone. The underlying message has to be: 'Shape what you can, limit the impact of what you can't'.

Given free rein, the Culture can shape a person's means and methods of communicating ideas, decision making, meeting habits and the manner in which people are reprimanded or left alone. If people are consistently political, lazy, recalcitrant, bullying, evasive, pessimistic, defeatist, alarmist, conservative and disloyal, it cannot be prescribed to personal nature alone but from cultural reinforcement. If Managers act in a way that is defensive and less than ambitious, it is usually from inadvertent education. It is not accidental – it is not the result of a set of unfortunate circumstances. It becomes established and conventional. 'Pockets' of ill-discipline tend to be pervasive – the lack of discipline in one place is seen elsewhere, albeit in different guises. The consequence of one act reverberates elsewhere. A damp patch in the ceiling does not mean everywhere else is dry. As previously mentioned, in any organisation no man is, or can be, an island.

A bad attitude is the worst thing that can happen to a group of people. It's infectious. Roger Allen Raby

It is easy to underestimate the entrenching qualities of bad attitudes – they shape cultures and by definition, the way that people behave. They are like ditches on the roadside: easy to drive into and very difficult to get out of. And the new incumbent who wants to shift those attitudes has a fight on their hands. They are values that have been enforced for a reason. When the new starter queues up to clock out along with everyone else it is certainly not through their own initiative; it is not from a sudden eagerness to get home; it is not done as an insult nor is it done to 'test' procedure. It becomes part of the organisational curriculum, the unofficial but effective lessons that are a necessary part of their education - and the part they play only strengthens and reinforces the culture that is allowed to permeate. It is neither scientific nor complicated – but is rarely analysed and dealt with. Attacking bad attitudes as they occur is like sweeping up pollution on the beach without looking at where the rubbish is coming from

Rules, custom and practice in an organisation's culture leave an indelible mark that enforce traditions and accepted codes of practice that are neither spoken nor written down. They become mythological. The things you *must* or *must not* do are enshrined in an unsung folklore – and like all folklore they are historical, buried in half-truths, embellished and always difficult to find a first-hand account. I was once told that a Manager threw himself across the bonnet of a car in a mad attempt to get people to stay and work overtime – such was the pressure and misguided belief that life itself depended on getting the orders out that particular day. It was a story that was banded about, supporting the perception that Management was desperate, out of control and inconsiderate. On further investigation, it turned out to be one solitary Manager who, many years earlier, clearly unhinged and unthinking, made a bit of a fool of himself. Hardly the stuff of a deep-seated cultural debility -mostly a one-off misjudgement. But how people milked it! How that Manager was used as the 'pin-up' boy for the uncaring, aloof attitude of the Management team.

And yet, some Managers can take sole responsibility for maintaining and shoring up cultural mores and attitudes that pervade the rest of the organisation. I remember one Director who wanted to remove some of the 'sacred cows' that were impeding the organisation and implement some real cultural changes. When it was suggested he should give up his own, private parking place next to the main door, he went absolutely berserk: "I want to make changes in this organisation - but not that one!" A Sales Director purchased an extremely large, leather-cushioned office chair which, in the confines of his office looked quite imposing. When his sales assistants asked whether they could buy new chairs (many were broken – their job was to sit there all day and answer calls) they were eventually given permission to buy much cheaper ones. "Well", the Director said, "we couldn't afford to buy everyone a chair like mine!"

Choices

Should we be in a position to say: this is what I want *and need* but that option is not open to everyone else? When written down, the thought sounds ridiculous: I need a bigger, more comfortable and expensive chair because I have more responsibility? The majority would recoil at such a suggestion but it is an easy trap in which to fall. The flexible hours, the parking place, the bigger desk, the better screen, the bigger window and the bigger office all become transparent perks and are noisy blasts of hierarchy amid the whispers of 'engagement'. The trapping of a 'Directors Only' canteen may well belong to a not-too-distant past but the distinctions and demarcations still exist. It does not entirely discredit the ideals of 'inclusion' but it becomes a much more difficult policy to preach. If the Director has a labelled car parking space, why not the Machine Operator, the Line Leader, the Quality Inspector, the Receptionist? I have never experienced someone from the shopfloor being invited to the golf day; it is not often people from the production lines are taken on factory tours. People in offices are given coffee as a matter of course, people on the shopfloor have to take money from their own pocket. If free samples are available, word is always given to the office staff before any notice is given to the people producing them. 'Engagement' and the unwillingness of people to subscribe to this ideology it is not always about what Managers covet and obtain, it is about those things that are *denied* to others.

And this can be at the very core of how a culture is shaped, engineered and sustained. Once achieving a position of responsibility and authority it is difficult to devalue its importance but can be at odds with the mantra of engagement and team-spirit. A Manager should not be beguiled by edifices and symbols of stature. *The addition of new equipment does not make a better Manager any more than a style makeover makes a person 'better'.* Some see it as a mark of credibility and of their hard-earned status, others as a right or tradition passed on from others. Whilst understandable, they are demeaning and unnecessary. It is wide open to the accusation of hypocrisy: of demanding the need of a team ethos and creating less distance in the organisation at the same time as propping up the totems that say something quite different. We live in an age when free tickets are given to those who are best available to afford them; ludicrously expensive free 'tasters' are given to the famously rich and doors are always opened to dignitaries and royalty. The difference within any organisation, is that Managers and Leaders have the ability, authority and responsibility to dismiss these social anomalies; a Manager can substantiate his or her statements on their 'greatest asset' and really influence how the social norms in the organisation are constructed, perceived and established.

This is the true essence of the culture within any business, large or small. Whilst we are never good judges of our own behaviour, it is difficult to assess the great storm of perceptions that are created by even the smallest actions and beliefs. These in turn are caused by the interpretation of one's own role and responsibilities and ultimately our understanding of status, hierarchy and power. *Who created this culture? You did. We did.*

Are we nearly there, yet?

Have I have painted a rather dystopian view of the business world? The challenger might well advocate that if it is true, how is it that organisations work? How is it that many are profitable? Why is it that many are excellent places to work that consistently offer great products to the ultimate satisfaction of the paying customer? My premise is not that organisations are on the brink of collapse but that they could be so much better. So many organisations regardless of their faults, weaknesses and frailties, are only a few steps away from being 'great'. Only a few changes with far reaching consequences need to be made that could shape any organisation from being 'good' to 'excellent'.

Organisations are not necessarily dysfunctional but fail to use the sources of potential and success they have within easy reach. This is partly because the ideas of good Management still lie in the maxims of: PLANNING; ORGANISING; DIRECTING AND CONTROLLING. With this philosophy, it is no wonder that people get the wrong idea. But these ideas are still peddled, still studied and indoctrinated like a Managerial panacea.

I have met so many Executives, Directors, Managers, Supervisors and Team Leaders over the years. I have many good ones but not many that are truly 'great'. This is *not* generated from an unhealthy inclination to criticise but from a sense of frustration. There are so many I have met who could be *really* good or *really* great but due to circumstances, insecurity, politics, ambition and misunderstanding, they search for what is considered best whilst knowing it is either wrong or counter-productive. So many want to hear their own voices rather than others; so many want the world to know how clever they are without understanding how clever the those around them are; so many want to offer a solution before even asking whether one is already in place; so many want to bolster their status - and by their very actions, undermine it.

Getting back to basics can be a fundemental change in itself – as long as people understand what those basics are and ensuring that people understand the implications of re-affirming the grounding tenets of the work, the job, and the business. Improvements in systems, processes, the environment, the structure and people require a change – a change in what people 'do'. Our behaviour is 'shaped' by systems, processes, environment, structure and people but equally, systems, processes, environment, structure - and those around us - are a direct consequence of *our* behaviour. Changing behaviour will, by definition, change the surrounding environment. Change the environment and you change behaviour, not only in yourself but in others. Instead of falling victim to circumstance and conditions, it is important to take charge of these 'shapers' within the environment and the resulting and contributory behaviours. These 'shapers' are the very elements and principles by which people can manage, influence and change the way the organisation works. They are the fundamentals by which an ordinary Company can become 'great' and a 'great' Company can become 'world-class'. Shaping the basics - and the behaviours around them - can shift the mediocre organisation to being a 'Centre of Excellence'. 'World Class' is about how people in an organisation work together. In essence 'World Class', like the pervasive, ubiquitous phrase, 'Culture', is how people think and what people 'do'.

The point is, if organisations use substantially less than the potential of Employees, how can they claim they are centres of excellence, that they are fantastically efficient and that they cannot be improved? Well, they can't. Complacency, assumptions, and a consistent lack of discipline so often get in the way. This leads to a lack of constructive challenge based on a common failure to appreciate the strength and potential of the people in the organisation. They lie at the core of most organisation's failure to be world class and by their very breadth and scope are difficult to identify. The accepted mores and practices within any organisation act as blinkers to a stream of possibilities. The moment an Employee walks through the main door of any business, the only features that are noticed are those that are completely different to the norm. This is not a biased assessment, just an accepted acknowledgement of how we are. We all have our adopted predilections, prejudices and opinions that are hard to break. Try telling the Manager that the grumbling and belligerent Employee really has a point to make and is actually trying to do a good job; try telling the stressed Supervisor that his or her team are not trying to make things difficult but probably don't understand what is expected of them; try telling the HR person conducting the second or third disciplinary that inside the person in front of them, is a talented individual trying to get out. Only by radically altering the conditions do a lot of other factors come to light. Which is why change is so important and why that change has to be substantial to make any real and lasting difference.

It is easier for an outsider to see the potential. It is easier to see other people's purpose, strengths and weaknesses, abilities, level of confidence and potential. Nine tenths of consultancy work is the ability to have an objective eye - the rest is articulating what is seen. And what is seen is not marvellous theory, left-of-field ideas and world-shattering visions but simple truths and simple solutions.

The day is not far off when the economic problem will take the back seat where it belongs, and the arena of the heart and the head will be occupied or reoccupied, by our real problems — the problems of life and of human relations of creation and behaviour... John Maynard Keynes

If Keynes statement has a utopian ring then it is only because there are so many waiting for it to happen, as opposed to creating the much needed circumstances. Sadly the economic conditions will continue to prevail and before anything changes the powers of the Manager will dictate the livelihoods and well-being of a substantial number of well-meaning, hard-working individuals who desire only a few things: a viable job, some responsibility and reward, some recognition, some direction and a helping hand. There is a long way to go. The job is easy enough but the wretched complications for which we are all guilty, make it ever more difficult.

The Essential Obligation

We all learn that after many years, what we know can be written on an ever decreasing size of stamp. It is a sign of learning, not of ignorance; a sign of experience rather than naivety. Often, it is a matter of perspective: sometimes the horizon becomes wider, more expansive and what we know shrinks in comparison. Other times, the necessary pieces of the jigsaw – what we need to know – becomes less complicated and less important. It is like a sculpture that is chiselled from an oversized, misshapen block of stone. The complications and contradictions of what we see, experience, touch and feel get hacked away until a simpler truth emerges. What we really need to know is simple. How to do it - and its constant application - is the hard bit.

There is an essential obligation and condition for any Manager's success. It is the ability to take the Company's best asset and instruct, inspire, develop and nurture them. And in accepting this proposition, it should be taken much more seriously than it is today. It starts with the recruitment process, the training and development, the search for ambition, motives and predispositions of any new, aspiring Employee, Supervisor or Manager. It sparks a different set of questions; it inspires new objectives and drives new ways of working and philosophies.

There is a responsibility here that is only fleetingly acknowledged or understood. Even when the worst Managers are finally dismissed, there appears to be no obligation to apologise to those who have endured the autocracy or disregard perpetuated for months or years; there is little willingness to understand the amount of damage that has been suffered or even visit the decisions that have been made. Instead, there is a rush to fill the gap without understanding the real imperatives and what is really required. The gaping vacancy should remain open until suitability meets potential and talent; when *willingness* meets *capability*.

The rush to hire should be tempered with the consequences of failure. By appointing or promoting a person who knowingly will alienate, limit and subjugate is to set the tone for the rest of the organisation and encompasses a considered determination to control and influence the talents and abilities of the departments they run.

The role of the Manager is an age from being confined to the bin of antiquity. However, within the role and duties of a Manager, there should be an acceptance and ambition of redundancy. Many of the problems that arise (the unwillingness to train and develop, delegate, challenge, change and improve) arise from an inclination to hang on to what is known and what is comfortable. The proposition that a Manager could possibly become superfluous is anathema. If you are managing the same department year after year, is that a sign that you are doing a good job or have not yet succeeded at all?

Driving along the road, at a steady pace, there are two things that can happen when you take your hands off the wheel: either the car lurches violently, creating chaos and mayhem or it carries on as though the hands were never needed in the first place. If Management is like driving, you know you have mastered the car – and the ability to drive - when you can lift your hands from the wheel and nothing untoward happens. If all hell breaks loose, it is back to the drawing board to try again

One of the *best* and most *deflating* experiences in Management is returning from an extended break to find that everything is working perfectly - as though the department has been completely unaware of your absence. It is a perfect mix of contradictions that plays havoc with a Manager's innate self-esteem. On reflection, it is not your weakness but the department's strength; it is not your inadequacy but the department's ability. Indeed, there is no better indication to seek pastures new. When the five minutes looking out of the window (one of the most underrated Management exercises ever invented) becomes twenty minutes or longer, it is time to move on. When the push to innovate becomes a project to keep yourself occupied, then the department does not need a Manager, it needs a caretaker.

After leaving an organisation it is quite natural and exciting to ask how the business is getting on in your absence. It is only when you leave that the ambitions and aspirations flood to the surface and the 'what ifs' and 'if only' stain the idealistic perception of what could have achieved. Should the legacy be that you are missed? That they would like nothing more for you to return? Or that you are not missed at all? That 'things are going really well, thanks!' or that 'all hell broke loose?' Is it not the case that any appeal for you to return is actually for you to finish the work you started? That the legacy left behind is a failed one? Is it not an plea to go back the way things were and an admission that the department is incapable and clueless? Much as it might feed the ego and appeals to the aura of personality, it is much more likely to be an affirmation that the administration, bureaucracy, organisation and paraphernalia of the day cannot maintain its steady course without your hand on the tiller. Bridles and reins are always needed when the horse does not know anything else.

Getting there...

From the writings and undisputed influence of people like Taylor there has been an inexorable wave of Management bureaucrats, auditors and accountants. Currently, our image of Bankers, Corporate leaders, politicians and officials has more than ever led us to question the capabilities of people with livelihoods, people and the nation's welfare in their hands. More and more we have started to question the integrity of people in charge and their worth. As someone recently commented, we are suspicious of Leaders, not just because we don't know what they do, we fear they don't know either. Actually, the point is that we are *convinced* they don't know what they are doing. There is enough evidence. How much more is needed?

The big questions are, 'Who is qualified?' 'What are the credentials required?' 'What do we look for and what do we insist upon?' 'What do we expect of others and what do we expect of ourselves?' In 2009, in the heat and turmoil of the banking crisis, I heard the following question: What is the difference between Fred Goodwin (former 'Sir' and CEO of RBS Banking Group) Alistair Darling (former Chancellor of the Exchequer in the UK) and Terry Wogan (Radio host on BBC 2). The answer was, only Terry Wogan had a Banking qualification. You can't help laugh but lord knows, it's not really funny.

And yet, things are about to change. Regardless of the staunchest conservative influences, the playing field on which organisations have dictated the rules, are now being re-shaped. The skills, disciplines and aptitude of a Manager will be tested even more as 'power', 'influence' and the hazy meritocracy of organisations begins to shift and waver. A Manager's traditional role may well be overtaken by technology – but so are the temptations to influence, divide and rule by other means. Emails are as much divisive as they are helpful, corporate communiques are overtaking the need to talk to people directly and data warehouse systems are flooding the pages of management reports making is less likely to understand what is going on. The credentials of any good Manager will shift and the ability to comprehend data and information quickly and absorb its likely consequence will be a deciding factor in their ability to be successful. Being able to Manage people may well become subservient to the ability to manage data – but this is the same mistake amplified and expressed by other means.

In the near future, there will still be a need to build solid foundations of trust, recognition and responsibility whereby people have the confidence to be creative, productive and experimental in pushing the boundaries of performance and excellence. Creating the conditions by which people in the organisation can thrive will still be the core element of the Manager's role even at the expense of their own well-being. The reverse is an all too familiar story of Managers using their Employees as convenient stepping-stones on the pathways of their careers.

The redemption of any Manager is how they are able to create those conditions by which people can succeed. The ability to communicate, honestly and directly can be the source of a Manager's success. Once this discipline is forgotten or relinquished, there is but a slippery path to a Manager's role being increasingly anachronistic and viewed as a superfluous investment in an organisation's march towards ever increasing levels of efficiency. The derogatory sounding 'Techno geek' and 'Nerd', might well be the new forces within an organisation; they may well be driving new solutions and as such may well be the most influential and valuable asset. However, they are not removed from the undeniable absolute that people want to be encouraged, understood, and recognised, to understand the part they have to play and to contribute not only to their own success but that of others.

When the aspirations of many are still governed by the few and the hopes and dreams are governed by even fewer, it is difficult to imagine a world where those hopes and aspirations will ever be fulfilled. Great leaders are those whom many will follow, whether their purpose is for evil or good. People see the vision of what Leaders want, encapsulated and articulated in a person they will follow and obey. It is the responsibility of any Manager and Leader not to betray the trust and authority bestowed on them by their position and allow people an opportunity to chase their own aspirations – rather than the solitary purpose of the one in charge. At work, in Management, in life itself, there is nothing worse than the inability to make the best of the steady stream of available potential. That potential lies in relationships, in people's hands, hearts and minds. Harnessed properly, every industry would be a success, every person would be happier and most people would have a smile on their face. The trek to the office in the morning would look and feel very different indeed. And if a Manager can do this, then they have succeeded. Success - the 'destination' of any Manager - is not about meticulously playing the role in a uniform pattern of tedium and repetitiveness. There has to be a goal, an ambition and an 'end-game'. Getting *there*, in its absolute form is not having to manage at all.

ABOUT THE AUTHOR

Born in Manchester in 1958, Stephen F. Green has spent his working life in the UK and Denmark as a Change Consultant, Operations Director and as an Interim Manager. He has delivered numerous Change programmes, assignments and projects as well as carrying out permanent and interim roles in Companies as wide-ranging as HBOS, British Aerospace, Lemvigh-Müller Group, Burberry, Boots, Legal & General; Harper Collins; EEB; Arvin Cheswick; Boots; British Steel; Bernard Matthews; APV; Norcross; Beatson Clark; Ethel Austin; United Biscuits; Statoil; Aalborg Værft and within the Bakkavör Group.

Stephen Green currently resides in Berwick-upon-Tweed.

www.ingramcontent.com/pod-product-compliance
Lightning Source LLC
Chambersburg PA
CBHW051642170526
45167CB00001B/302